The Pitman Motorists' Library

The Book of the
IMPS

A practical handbook covering the Hillman Imp,
Singer Chamois, Sunbeam Stiletto, and
all Imp derivants to 1971

JOHN THORPE

Pitman Publishing

First published as The Book of the Hillman Imp and Singer Chamois, 1966
Second edition, as The Book of the Imps, 1972

SIR ISAAC PITMAN AND SONS LTD
Pitman House, Parker Street, Kingsway, London, WC2B 5PB
P.O. Box 46038, Portal Street, Nairobi, Kenya

SIR ISAAC PITMAN (AUST.) PTY. LTD
Pitman House, 158 Bouverie Street, Carlton, Victoria 3053, Australia

PITMAN PUBLISHING COMPANY S.A. LTD
P.O. Box 11231, Johannesburg, S. Africa

PITMAN PUBLISHING CORPORATION
6 East 43rd Street, New York, N.Y. 10017, U.S.A.

SIR ISAAC PITMAN (CANADA) LTD
495 Wellington Street West, Toronto 135, Canada

THE COPP CLARK PUBLISHING COMPANY
517 Wellington Street West, Toronto 135, Canada

ISBN: 0 273 36175 9

Printed by photo-lithography and
made in Great Britain at the Pitman Press, Bath
G2—(G4196:15)

Preface

As is my custom, before writing this book—intended to supplement not supplant your Owner's Handbook—I purchased a Hillman Imp so that I would be able to base my advice on first-hand knowledge of the vehicle. Consequently, much of the practical material in the book stems from my experiences. At the same time, I have become very conscious of the limitations which this brilliant small car places upon the owner who wants to do his own repairs.

There are some jobs which you can tackle and so save yourself both time and money. There are other jobs which you can tackle, but which will consume so much of your time that frankly the saving is not worthwhile. And there are still others which you cannot attempt at all—if you are wise—without possessing such a battery of special tools that the entire project would become utterly uneconomic. Where this is so—where, in my estimation, there is no worthwhile saving to be made in time or cash—I have said as much. And where there is a danger that attempting a job with inadequate tools could lead to costly damage I have noted that the job is beyond the average owner. For details of these refer to the Workshop Manual. Here I thank Chrysler (UK) Ltd. for their kind permission to use illustrations from that source.

For the rest, I have gone into as much detail as I have found to be necessary for the work in hand to be done. I do not advise that you should carry out complicated mechanical jobs with a spanner in one hand and this book in the other. That sort of an approach leads to trouble. Settle down comfortably, read the relevant chapter, and from it compile brief working notes if you feel that your memory will need to be jogged. But above all remember that your Imp will best repay meticulous attention to routine servicing. Major overhauls are a last resort, not a first essential. Bear that in mind, and you will enjoy small-car motoring at its best— behind the wheel of a well-tuned and reliable Imp or Singer Chamois.

JOHN THORPE

IMP DE LUXE

SUPER IMP

Contents

	Preface	iii
1	Make it routine	1
2	Tools and their use	12
3	Diagnosing faults	15
4	Top overhauls	28
5	Major overhauls	43
6	Work on the electrics	56
7	The cooling system	69
8	The fuel system and carburettors	74
9	Steering, suspension, wheels	95
10	The braking system	102
11	Work on the body	109
	Appendix	116
	Index	121

SINGER CHAMOIS

SUNBEAM STILETTO

SUNBEAM SPORT

1 Make it routine

PROPERLY driven and well maintained an Imp should cover a good 40,000 miles before the engine need be stripped. Up to that time only one decoke should have been needed. But if the routine maintenance has been neglected or skimped the overall mileage may be drastically shortened and its cost increased.

The reason is simple enough. Maladjustments have a cumulative effect. Little harm is likely to result, for instance, if a car covers a few miles with a faulty plug. But if thousands of miles are covered in such a condition because the owner forgot to check the state of his plugs at regular intervals all sorts of troubles may result. Local overheating, for example, can actually burn a hole right through the piston. At best, one cylinder is never operating at anything like its full power. Fuel consumption rises and the car's performance gradually falls off. And when at last the fault is discovered the owner may find that adjustment will no longer provide a cure. Instead he needs to have an expensive overhaul—with perhaps a new piston—to make good the result of neglecting to make a regular plug check. Is it worth it?

Consider the brakes. Here deterioration is constant, but so gradual that you tend to adjust yourself imperceptibly to the lessening power of the brakes in everyday driving. But emergencies do *not* adjust themselves and the day may come when you need to stop quicker than you have ever done before. And what do you find? Brakes, which six months before would have done it easily, are now no longer efficient enough. This lesson can be effective, providing you survive to appreciate it. Yet a set brake test carried out once a week as a matter of routine would ensure that you *know* what the condition of the "anchors" is.

TASK SYSTEMS

Constant and methodical inspection is the best way of preventing any such troubles but the usual recommendations—based on elapsed mileages —are difficult to carry out if a full log of work done is not kept. This was a problem which the Services had to face long ago, and one answer was the Task System. This called for daily and weekly checks as a matter of routine.

Modified, such a system is ideally suited for a privately-maintained car.

And here I have detailed two routines—one daily and one weekly—either of which could be employed by the average Imp owner. They cover all the more essential check points, and to carry them out need take no more than, on average, ten minutes a day or an hour each weekend.

Daily Task System. *Sunday*. Check adjustment of brakes; check hydraulic fluid level; check action of handbrake; check security of nuts and

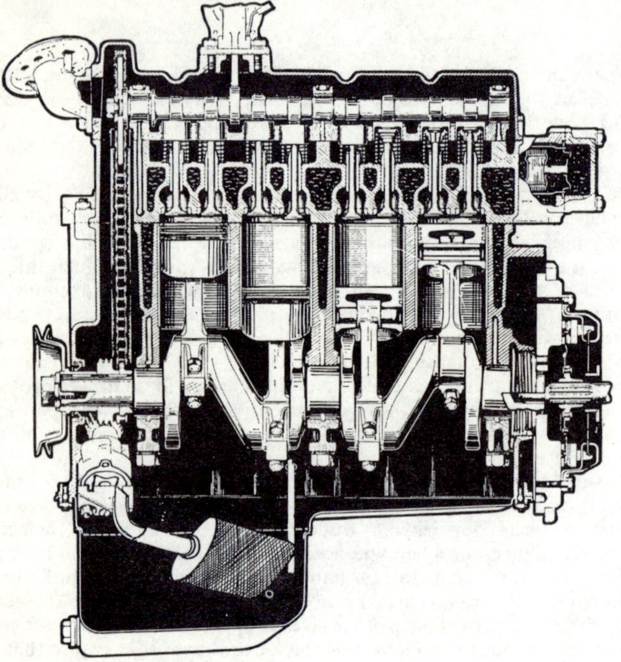

FIG. 1. SECTIONAL VIEW OF THE ENGINE

This longitudinal section through the power unit emphasizes its basic simplicity of design and construction and shows its main components.

bolts and unions in braking system; check lubrication of brake linkages; test security of back plates.

Monday. Check oil level in sump; check battery electrolyte; check coolant level in radiator; check all controls for adjustment and free movement; check tyre pressures.

Tuesday. Check all exposed electrical wiring for signs of abrasion or fracture; check terminals for security; check operation of lamps.

Wednesday. Examine tyre treads and remove any trapped stones; check walls for cracks; test tyre pressures; check wheels for security; check steering backlash.

Thursday. Check action of clutch; check brakes for distance to stop from 30 m.p.h., using known reference points.

Friday. Check all exposed nuts and bolts; bounce car to test dampers.

Saturday. Listen to tick-over and adjust if necessary; check contact-breaker gap; check plugs for condition and gap; check fan belt.

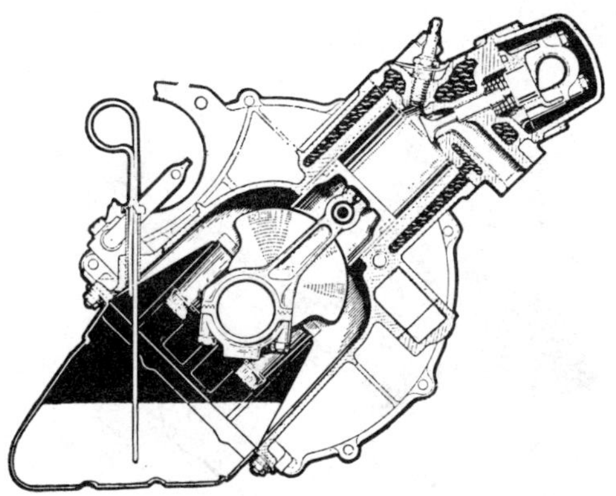

FIG. 2. THE CYLINDER AND CYLINDER HEAD LAYOUT

The engine cross-sectioned to reveal one cylinder and the crankshaft shown here at b.d.c., with one valve slightly open.

Alternative Weekly System. *Week* 1. Check adjustment of brakes; check hydraulic fluid level; check action of handbrake; test security of nuts and bolts and unions in the braking system; check lubrication of brake linkages; test security of back plates; test brakes for distance to stop from 30 m.p.h. using known reference points; check tyre pressures.

Week 2. Check oil level in sump; check battery electrolyte; check coolant level in radiator; check all controls for adjustment and free movement; examine tyre treads and remove trapped stones; examine side walls; check tyre pressures.

Week 3. Check all exposed electrical wiring for signs of abrasion or fracture; check all terminals for security; check operation of lamps; check tyre pressures; check oil and coolant levels.

Week 4. Check all nuts and bolts for security; bounce car to test action of dampers; check steering backlash; listen to tick-over and adjust if necessary; check contact-breaker gap; check plugs for condition and gap; test fan belt play; test tyre pressures.

By employing a daily approach to routine maintenance you will ensure that most of the major points are checked at least once a week. Even allowing for a pretty substantial use of the car this should mean that no fault should go undetected for more than 500 miles, and most defects would be discovered almost before they have had time to develop.

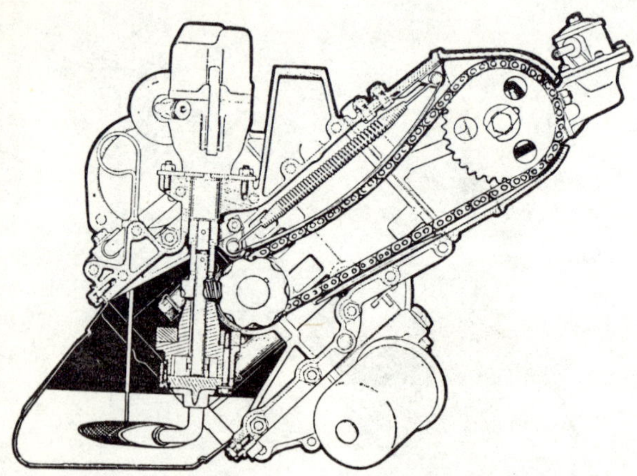

FIG. 3. THE OIL PUMP, DISTRIBUTOR, AND CAMSHAFT DRIVES

One single skew gear on the crankshaft, as this drawing clearly shows, drives the oil pump and distributor; an automatically tensioned chain drives the overhead camshaft.

With the weekly system, of course, there is a greater time-lag though one or two points are double-checked during the period. Where the car is used mainly as a weekend runabout the time-lag does not assume a great significance, but if the monthly mileage is much in excess of 500 then it would be better to make the checks on a daily rather than a weekly basis.

Note though that the idea is to *check* the relevant items, not necessarily to carry out any adjustments. Where the routine examination discloses no faults then no actual work need be carried out.

LUBRICATION

Obviously, the system of checks does not take into account either seasonal or periodic jobs such as oil changes and greasing. These must still be done on an elapsed mileage basis, and a record should be kept of the date and the mileage reading at which each service was made.

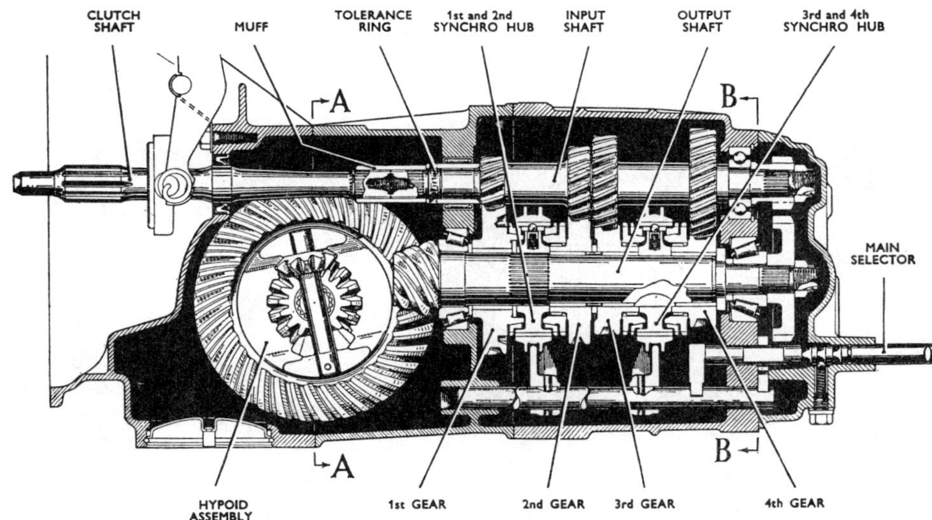

Fig. 4. The Transaxle

Although seemingly one unit, the transaxle is actually split at A–A and B–B. From left to right, the first section contains the differential; the second the gearbox proper; and the third the reverse and selector mechanisms.

As memory can be notoriously fickle it is no bad plan to have a reminder actually on the car itself. I find that one of the best methods is to stick a small strip of self-adhesive coloured tape to the underside of the bonnet. This is bound to catch the eye. On it jot down either the date and mileage at which, for instance, the oil was last changed, or the mileage at which it is next due for a change. But be sure to use one system only and stick to it.

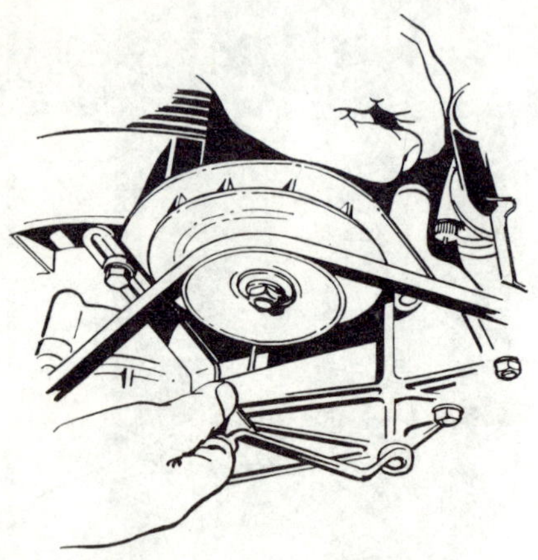

FIG. 5. THE WATER PUMP BRACKET

During routine maintenance keep an eye on the security of the nuts which hold the pump/fan assembly to the engine. Use a torque wrench, if you have one, and set the tension to the correct figure (*see* page 119).

It is a great mistake to neglect these periodic lubrication sessions. The engine oil contained in the sump is constantly circulated through the power unit. In time it becomes dirty—contaminated with minute pieces of metal worn from the pistons, rings, and bores, and mixed with water and petrol which percolate down from the cylinders. Remember that for each gallon of fuel burned in the engine rather more than a gallon of water is produced. Much of this finds its way out of the exhaust pipe in the form of vapour—you have probably noticed how much steam is emitted from the exhaust pipe on a cold morning just after the engine has started. But some of it condenses on the cylinder bores and runs down the walls into the sump. Left to itself, this will form sludge. And, of course, the net result of all this is to lessen the oil's lubricating properties.

Topping-up the Oil Sump. Never neglect this simple maintenance job. It is advisable to withdraw the dipstick once a week (more often if a big mileage is covered) and check that the oil level in the sump is in accordance with the correct level mark. If it is not, top-up with one of the summer or winter grade Shell engine oils recommended in the Appendix on page 116.

How to Change the Oil. It is useless to try to make an oil change with the engine cold because the dirty oil will not flow properly. Instead let the unit warm up first—better still, go for a few miles' motoring first—and

FIG. 6. RENEWING THE OIL FILTER ELEMENT

The filter is reached from underneath the car. Change the filter element each time you change the engine oil. Unscrew the filter bowl from its housing, withdraw and discard the used filter element, flush out the housing, and then fit a new filter element. When reassembling, make sure that the seal between the bowl and the housing is perfect.

then place your drain tray under the unit. Take off the oil filler-cap to obviate any suction effect. Remove the sump drain plug and the oil will gush out, carrying with it most of the impurities contained in the sump.

Replace the drain plug and pour in flushing oil. Run the engine for a further five minutes—at a standstill this time—to circulate the oil. This clean light lubricant will wash away any deposits in the oil channels and galleries.

Stop the engine, allow a few minutes for the flushing oil to drain back into the sump, and then remove the drain plug again and leave the car for a while so that all the flushing oil runs away. Jack up the front to flush oil out of the valve compartment. Renew the filter. Then, with the car level, pour in fresh engine oil until the correct level on the dipstick is reached.

Check the oil level again after your first trip and top up if necessary. Do not mix different grades of oil. Those specified in the Appendix to this book are arrived at after much careful experimental work on the part of the Chrysler factory. You will not be able to improve on their results and

you may easily take thousands of miles off the life of your engine by trying
to do so.

Transaxle Oil. The level of the oil in the gearbox—which also serves
the transaxle—should be checked at intervals of 5,000 miles. To do so,
remove the filler-cum-level plug located high up on the side of the transaxle, forward of the drive shafts, on the left-hand side of the car. The level
should be just up to the filler orifice. If it is not, top it up. This can be
done quite easily by using a plastic "squeezy" bottle. Clean it thoroughly,
fill it with the correct grade of oil, and attach a plastic hose to the top of
the bottle. By squeezing the bottle, the oil can be pumped into the
transaxle.

At 15,000-mile intervals the transaxle should be drained and refilled
with fresh oil. Do this when the unit is still hot, after a run. Then remove
the filler plug and the drain plug—this is set lower down and slightly to
the rear. Let all the old oil drain away, replace the drain plug, and refill
with fresh oil. Here, again, the "squeezy" bottle will come in useful.
Finally, replace and tighten the filler plug.

TAPPETS

Tappet Adjustment. On the Imp the tappet clearances are adjusted by
varying the size of shim used between the valve and the cam follower. This
is done only after major overhauls, not as a matter of routine. The method
is fully detailed on pages 32, 39 and 40.

THE CONTACT-BREAKER

Every 5,000 miles (or twice a year at least) the contact-breaker gap must
be checked and the points examined. To do this release the two spring
clips which hold the distributor cap and detach it. Then grasp the rotor
arm and pull it upwards to remove it, so giving access to the points. You
will need to turn the engine over, so it is advisable to remove the sparking
plugs too. They can be checked at the same time.

Rotate the crankshaft until the contact-breaker points are seen to be
fully open. Insert a 0·015 in. feeler gauge. This should just fit. If insertion
of the gauge forces the points further apart adjustment will be needed. If,
on the other hand, you feel no resistance at all as the gauge is inserted
make a second check with, say, a 0·018 in. feeler. Should this be accepted
the gap will have to be decreased.

Before making any adjustment ensure that the point faces are not
dirty, burned, nor pitted. If they are, new points may be needed—or at
least the existing ones will have to be refaced.

Setting the Contact-breaker Gap. Remove the distributor cap and pull
off the rotor arm. Then turn the engine over until the fibre heel of the
moving points arm comes on to the peak of one of the distributor cams

and fully opens the gap between the contact-breaker points. Measure this with a feeler gauge. It should be 0·015 in. If it is not correct, adjustment is needed.

With a screwdriver, loosen the single screw which locks the fixed contact plate to the distributor base. Do not free it completely. The plate should be movable, but not loose. Now insert a 0·015 in. feeler gauge into the gap and keep it there while you insert the screwdriver into the adjuster slot on the plate. By twisting the screwdriver the gap between the points can be varied. When the feeler can just, but only just, be slipped back and forth between the points, tighten the clamping screw again.

A rare ignition fault is that the distributor shaft may be bent. This can lead to uneven firing. A ready check on this is to measure the contact-breaker gap with the heel of the arm on the peak of each cam in turn. Any significant variation suggests a shaft out of true, and the distributor should then be stripped and a new shaft inserted.

Re-gapping the Sparking Plugs. Difficult starting or occasional misfiring can often be traced to dirty or incorrectly gapped sparking plugs. The life of a good sparking plug such as the Champion N9Y (recommended by Chrysler) is considerable, but the points of the electrodes gradually burn away, causing the gap between them to become excessive. It is then necessary to re-gap the plug.

It is advisable to check the gap between the electrodes of the four K.L.G. sparking plugs fitted to the Imp cylinder head about once a month or about every 2,000 miles and to re-gap each sparking plug if the gap exceeds 0·025 in. This is the gap recommended by the makers of the Imp. Check the gap with a suitable feeler gauge and re-gap the plug *after* cleaning if this is necessary. The feeler gauge should just slide between the plug points without springing them.

When adjusting the plug gap never attempt to bend or tap the centre electrode. Use a pair of snipe-nosed pliers, or preferably a plug re-gapping tool, to bend the outside (earth) electrode. Before replacing each sparking plug, renew the copper washer at its base if this is found to be worn or flattened, and clean the plug threads with a wire brush. Screw the plug home by hand as far as possible, and always use a box spanner for final tightening. Never use an adjustable spanner as this is liable to cause distortion. Be careful to connect the distributor leads to the correct sparking plugs. Each lead is marked.

Engine Additives. A considerable range of additives, both for petrol and oil, has been marketed in recent years. It is now generally acknowledged that some beneficial results may be obtained by employing them, but claims sometimes tend to be over-optimistic.

I have found REDeX to be, generally, the most useful additive and I always make a point of using it during running-in, both in the petrol and in the oil. On older engines, injecting a small quantity of REDeX direct into the carburettor intake with the engine running will often free gummed rings or sticky valves. In my opinion, a shot of this additive with every gallon of petrol is an insurance against excessive engine wear, and REDeX's "home dispenser" makes it easy to administer from bulk supplies.

BRAKE ADJUSTMENT

To compensate for wear in the linings one must alter the position of the brake shoes relative to the drum, and this is done by means of adjusters located on the respective brake backplates. Each rear brake has one adjuster only; but the double-leading-shoe front brake has two adjusters. The method of adjustment is fully detailed on pages 104–5.

The Handbrake. The method of resetting this control is also described under the appropriate heading in Chapter 10.

ADJUSTING THE FAN BELT

Remember to check the fan belt adjustment regularly, for it drives the dynamo and the water pump as well as the fan. Set it so that there is half an inch of free play when the belt is tested in the centre. Too much play will cause slip; too tight a belt may snap (*see* also Fig. 5).

CHASSIS GREASING

Kingpin Lubrication. Early Hillman Imp and Singer Chamois cars had no greasing points at all. This was altered, in 1966, by the inclusion of a total of four grease nipples for the steering.

All of these are located on the kingpins—two nipples on each side. Every 5,000 miles it is essential to deliver two pumps of a grease gun to each of these nipples. The manufacturers recommend the use of Shell Multi-purpose Chassis Grease, or any equivalent grade produced by other makers.

Running-in a new or reconditioned engine. No matter how accurate the machining, new parts are by no means absolutely smooth. The profile of a gear tooth—for instance—seen through the microscope looks like a view of the Himalayas. Only use can grind away these minute high spots, and until the various parts have bedded down the engine will be stiff and will not be capable of developing its full power. Unless carefully run-in an engine can be permanently spoiled.

Therefore, with a new or rebuilt engine keep to the maximum speeds set out below. But don't take them too literally. They should not be exceeded, but equally one should not try to labour up a gradient at 20 m.p.h. in top gear when 20 m.p.h. in third would be more appropriate. The engine must never be overloaded—which is just what tackling too steep a gradient in too high a gear does—just as it must never be over-revved. Either course is injurious. Aim, instead, to keep the engine turning over easily and smoothly all the time—and don't be afraid of the gear lever.

You may find it necessary to increase the tick-over speed slightly, too, to get reliable idling. This is because the greater internal friction leads to slower-than-normal running at low throttle openings.

Change the oil and the filter after the first 500 miles on the road, and again at the 1,000-mile mark. Don't use any additives in the engine other than upper-cylinder lubricant or, possibly, plain graphite. Molybdenum disulphide has a very powerful "plating" action and if it is used at this stage there is a danger that the parts will never get properly run in at all.

Remember, too, that with a new car the transmission will remain relatively stiff for about 2,000 miles. Try, therefore, to use the gears as much as possible so that all the pinions get a reasonable chance to bed down properly.

PERMISSIBLE MAXIMUM SPEEDS WHEN RUNNING-IN A
NEW CAR OR RECONDITIONED ENGINE

Mileage covered	Max. in first	Max. in second	Max. in third	Max. in top
Up to 500 miles	10 m.p.h	18 m.p.h.	30 m.p.h.	40 m.p.h.
500 miles to 1,000 miles	15 m.p.h.	27 m.p.h.	45 m.p.h.	60 m.p.h.

2 Tools and their use

It is a mistake to attempt to maintain or overhaul a car with inadequate tools—especially a car like the Imp which has many light-alloy components. To undertake even routine maintenance jobs calls for the use of a good-quality tool kit, while major overhauls can quite often require the use of special Service Tools designed by the car manufacturer to do one specific job and one only.

Every new car, when delivered, is equipped with a standard tool kit. Save for a few items this kit is intended only for dealing with roadside emergencies; it is very definitely *not* sufficient for sterner work. The need for special service tools for undertaking certain jobs is dictated solely because many mechanical parts are made to precision-engineering standards and therefore some of the assembly work is such that once the components have been assembled at the factory, only special tools have the slightest chance of safely freeing and subsequently assembling the parts concerned.

Even where the jobs to be tackled do not call for the use of special service tools, they still require the use of *good* tools. The purchase of cheap tools is always a bad investment, for besides not wearing as well as they should, they also have an infuriating habit of ruining nuts and bolts.

TOOLS YOU NEED

The first essential is to buy a really good set of chrome-vanadium open-ended spanners in A/F sizes. A set of six double-ended spanners will give a range of sizes sufficient for most work, and should cost only a couple of pounds.

Next, it is essential to obtain a set of strong box spanners or, better still, a set of socket spanners. I would also not be without my set of ring spanners which, though less handy for use in confined spaces than open-ended or socket spanners, enable a very good grip to be obtained with no danger of the spanner slipping.

For serious work a torque wrench should be available. Almost every nut and bolt on the car has an accurate lb ft torque setting specified (*see* Appendix, page 119–20). Using a torque wrench is the only way to ensure that you get these settings correct.

Almost equally essential are a pair of really good screwdrivers with insulated handles. One screwdriver with a $\frac{5}{16}$ in. blade and an electrical screwdriver with a $\frac{1}{8}$ in. blade are the minimum requirements. Two cross-head screwdrivers (large and small) are essentials.

You will also need a pair of pliers equipped with wire cutters. Pliers are indispensable for electrical and cable work. A set of small B.A. spanners is also useful for electrical jobs. Finally you will require a set of suitable feeler gauges for gap-setting the valve clearances, sparking plugs and contact-breaker, a good hammer, soft-metal drifts, one or two wire brushes, a scraper for decarbonizing, a valve spring compressor, and a valve grinding tool.

USING YOUR TOOLS

Casual selection of spanners, placing them in position and tugging hard may damage your engine. Each particular type of spanner has its own characteristics and is best suited for one particular type of job.

Open-ended Spanners. The great all-rounders are unquestionably the open-enders. These can be used in confined spaces and have the great advantage that their jaws are angled. This means that an open-ender can be used to loosen or tighten an awkwardly-situated nut and then, when the limit of movement has been reached, reversed to give fresh purchase. In this way it is possible to loosen or tighten an obstinate nut by easy stages.

It is, of course, essential that only the right size of spanner should be used. The open-ended spanner is designed to apply its pressure on the flats of a nut or bolt, and it is consequently made with jaws of just the right width to grip a certain head size. If a larger spanner is used, instead of gripping the flats the jaws will press against the angles of the nut or bolt. Then one of two things can happen. Either the spanner gouges away the angle of the nut or bolt, leaving a rounded head which no ordinary spanner can thereafter grip, or else the nut or bolt head slightly springs the jaws of the spanner, which is promptly ruined.

Damage to the spanner jaws can also be caused by applying excessive force when trying to free a nut or bolt which refuses to budge. There is a temptation, under these circumstances, to slip a piece of piping over the free end of the spanner to increase its leverage. Although this is permissible where due care is used, it is all too easy to apply excessive force and to spring the jaws of the spanner or snap a bolt or stud.

Ring, Box and Socket Spanners. These can be used to great advantage when really obstinate nuts or bolts have to be dealt with. Ring and socket spanners both grip on the angles, not on the flats. They are consequently able to apply pressure at half-a-dozen points where the open-ended spanner can only do so at two. Box spanners, provided they are stoutly constructed, go one stage better. A box spanner applies force at both angles and flats, all the way round the nut or bolt. Frequently, however, the tommy-bar used to turn a box spanner simply bends under the strain, or else the offset between the part of the spanner holding the nut or bolt and the tommy-bar hole, where the pressure is applied, tilts the spanner which then rides off the hexagon.

When using any type of spanner to tighten nuts or bolts it is important to remember that too much force should never be used. Spanners are made long enough to ensure that, for any given size nut or bolt, mere hand pressure applied through the full leverage of the spanner will tighten the nut or bolt adequately. If excessive force is used the actual material of a bolt can be weakened sufficiently to cause it to fracture. This point should also be borne in mind when tightening bolts which are threaded into a light-alloy component. Here the steel bolt is much harder than the material into which it is screwed, and over-enthusiasm with spanner application can easily strip the thread inside the hole.

Pliers. These, of course, should never be used as a makeshift spanner because their jaws can never be truly parallel, and the serrated grip is most perilously liable to slip. A rounded hexagon is the inevitable result if this occurs.

Screwdrivers. These should have their blades properly ground so that the blade (side view) is first concave and then runs parallel to the tip. This enables the blade to seat itself properly in the slot and to apply pressure which is evenly distributed. A screwdriver whose blade is wedge-shaped (side view) does not seat properly and instead of exerting an even pressure on the sides of the slot it exerts all its force on the edges which understandably tend to crumble under the strain.

Special Service Tools. Chrysler specify the use of special service tools for some operations. On the gearbox, for example, little or nothing can be done without them. Do not try because you will only damage your Imp. All the jobs covered in this book, unless otherwise stated, can, however, be done with the tools suggested above.

3 Diagnosing faults

WHEN a doctor wishes to diagnose a patient's illness he works methodically, listing the various symptoms to build up an overall picture of the complaint. This done he can usually identify it and give treatment accordingly. Exactly the same type of diagnosis has to be made in the case of an engine which refuses to work. Obviously there is a fault—some reason why it will not work—and before the fault can be cured it has got to be located and identified. The search for it must be as methodical as a doctor's approach.

If certain requirements are being properly fulfilled the engine must work. If it is not working it follows that one or more of these requirements is not being met. Fault diagnosis boils down to discovering which of them it is. An engine must work if the correct charge of petrol/air mixture is being sucked into the cylinders at the right time, properly compressed, fired at the right time, and the residues properly exhausted. The first stage in checking must, therefore, be the obvious one of checking that there is, in fact, an adequate supply of mixture reaching the cylinders.

Checking the Fuel System As an invariable first step, always check that there is sufficient petrol in the tank. Then comes the task of ascertaining that the petrol is reaching the carburettor. Flowing of the petrol could be prevented by a blockage in the petrol pipe, a faulty pump, a choked filter, or a jammed needle-valve in the float chamber. Detach the fuel pipe from the carburettor and operate the hand lever on the fuel pump. Petrol should spurt out. If it does the float chamber of the carburettor can be opened up for inspection. First, however, reconnect the pipe.

When the float chamber is open the pump may be operated again so that you can see whether or not the fuel is flowing past the needle valve properly. Also look for signs of dirt in the float chamber itself. If there is sediment on the bottom of it take the opportunity of swilling the chamber out thoroughly before everything is replaced.

Normally, this initial check on the fuel system takes only a few minutes. It will give one of two answers: either fuel is reaching the float chamber or it is not. If it is not you have found at least a contributory cause of the breakdown, and this should be rectified before proceeding further.

Suppose that no fuel flows through the pipe. This would indicate that the trouble lies somewhere between the free end of the pipe and the fuel tank—in the pipe itself, in the pump, or in the tank pick-up. In this case the next step is obviously to detach the pipe at the pump end and then to operate the pump. If no fuel emerges, then the obvious inference is that the pump filter itself is blocked with dirt or that the diaphragm is faulty. So the filter dome should be removed and the filter and pump checked.

It is possible for the fuel system to be at fault by supplying too much fuel as well as too little. Overflooding, as this form of trouble is called, is easily diagnosed. Fuel drips from the carburettor, and the engine, if it runs at all, constantly misfires and sounds distinctly "lumpy."

Unless pump pressure is wrong, only the float assembly can be responsible for this particular form of trouble. The float may be punctured, in which case it will simply sink to the bottom of the float chamber and allow the valve to remain open. More likely, however, is the ingress of dirt into the valve assembly. Even a tiny speck of hard matter is sufficient to prevent the needle from seating properly, and this keeps the valve partially open. The effect of this milder form of overflooding is most noticeable at low engine speeds where the excess of petrol is not being used up as quickly as at high engine speeds. Finally the float-chamber needle itself may have become bent. A thorough inspection of the float chamber assembly is the only way to diagnose the exact cause of the trouble.

Checking the Ignition System. Where the initial inspection of the fuel system shows no obvious fault the next stage of your diagnosing should be switched to the ignition system. First of all remove the four sparking plugs and inspect their electrode gaps. If inspection and checking with a feeler gauge shows that the gap for each plug is neither too closely nor too widely set, each plug in turn should be reconnected to its H.T. lead and then the metal body of the plug should be placed in contact with the cylinder head or some convenient metal part of the car in such a position that the spark gap can easily be seen.

With the ignition switched on, turn the engine over. As you do this a good spark should be seen and heard to jump across the gap between the plug electrodes. This check should be repeated several times and if no spark results, a brand new plug (this essential "spare" should always be carried) should be substituted for the old one, and the check repeated. If the new plug sparks and the old one fails to, then the obvious inference is that the old plug's insulation has broken down, and fitting a new plug in its place will cure the trouble. If, on the other hand, a new plug also fails to spark, the trouble lies somewhere between the sparking plug terminal and the battery, and a much more exhaustive check is needed. The battery, dynamo, coil, contact-breaker or distributor may be at fault.

Diagnosing Mechanical Trouble. Complete engine failure for any reason other than ignition or fuel trouble is unlikely, except in the somewhat remote event of such a vital part as the timing gear drive to the distributor being stripped. Other troubles, therefore, are likely to show themselves in reduced engine performance or erratic running.

One of the likelier causes of lack of pulling power is valve deterioration. Imp tappets are pre-set, and require no adjustment between overhauls. Thus any loss of compression is likely to indicate a valve fault. It is possible, where this is suspected, to diagnose where the fault lies from the way in which the engine behaves. If an inlet valve is not being properly closed there is a tendency for the engine to "spit back" through the carburettor, since some mixture will be driven back during the compression stroke. Where an exhaust valve is not seating properly the mixture tends to be driven into the exhaust system and to be ignited there by the heat, giving a constant banging or rumbling in the exhaust pipe.

A rough check can be made as follows. With the engine running, detach each ignition lead in turn. When the lead is taken off the cylinder which is *not* developing its full power the engine speed falls only slightly, but when the lead is removed from a cylinder which *is* contributing its full power the fall in engine speed is very marked, and the unit may even stop. Loss of compression can be caused by several faults besides valve trouble, but such faults are not commonly encountered. Distortion of the cylinder head joint, which could result if the engine is run when suffering from chronic overheating, is one example. This obviously calls for workshop treatment. In such a case there might be a distinct hiss of escaping gas audible at the joint all the time the engine is running, and since air would be induced into the cylinder, thus diluting the mixture, the engine would also tend to overheat. A leakage of coolant from the broken joint might also be noticeable.

Following a piston seizure (either through working the engine too hard before it was fully run-in or because of failure of the lubrication system) piston rings might be fractured. Besides losing compression, the engine might also begin to take oil into the combustion chambers. This oil, of course, would burn and the resulting smoke would issue from the exhaust pipe. When an engine loses power and smokes after a seizure the only wise course is to stop *immediately*, because the piston rings are almost certainly broken. Any further running might easily cause deep score marks on the cylinder bores where the broken ends of the rings act as efficient cutting tools, involving a major overhaul.

Faults in the Lighting System. Exactly the same process of elimination which is used for locating mechanical troubles is employed when diagnosing faults in the lighting system. Faced with electrical troubles, most laymen are completely nonplussed, but in actual fact electrical work is reasonably straightforward provided that the magic word "circuit" is borne in mind. Circuits are, in fact, the key to electricity. If electricity is present and the circuit is complete, the current *must* flow through it. If electricity is present but is not flowing, the circuit is not complete.

Faulty circuits are of two types—the open circuit and the short circuit. In the first case there is a break in the circuit and the wires on the far side of the break, viewed from the source, are dead. In the second case the current is still flowing but is following a *shorter* path to earth—as would be the case, for example, if one end of a live lead had become detached from its terminal and had earthed itself on the chassis.

Obviously the first essential is to be able to understand a wiring diagram (*see* Figs. 7–21). At first sight this may appear to be disconcertingly like a plan of a rather complicated suburban railway—and oddly enough it is not at all a bad idea to regard it in this light. If the various leads are thought of as railway tracks the whole idea becomes enormously simplified. It is as well to remember, however, that one important main line is not shown. This is the earth return. One terminal of the battery is connected straight to earth, and all the car components are similarly earthed. This, therefore, forms one complete half of the circuit.

To trace, for example, the circuit which lights the main headlamp bulb filament one takes as a starting point the unearthed terminal of the battery and follows the lead shown on the wiring diagram leading from this terminal. It goes to a point on the lighting switch. From the switch another lead is taken, through the dip switch, through the headlamp bulb, and thence to earth. If, therefore, the tumbler of the lighting switch connects these two main switch terminals there will be a complete circuit, for after passing through the filament the current returns via earth to the battery. Sometimes, where a rather more complicated circuit is involved, it helps to trace it out individually on a sheet of paper.

Having found the circuit, the next job is to check it. The first stage is to find out whether or not electricity is present, and here a spare bulb in a holder with a "wander" lead attached can be pressed into service. First, connect the bulb across the battery terminals. If the battery is in order the bulb will light. Once certain on this point it becomes necessary to check each individual lead in the circuit chosen. This is made considerably easier by the fact that each wire is given an outer casing of a different colour.

In the circuit used here as an example, the next step would be to lift out the lighting switch, complete with its leads, and to apply the lamp lead to the appropriate terminal while earthing the holder. Once again, the lamp should light, indicating that electricity is flowing as far as the terminal. The switch should then be set to the appropriate position and the check repeated on the second terminal. If that passes muster the next stage of the wiring—from the lighting switch to the dip switch—should be similarly checked. Finally the one remaining lead—from the dip switch to the headlamp bulb—should be tested. This assumes that one has examined the headlamp bulb first, to make sure its filament is intact!

When the faulty section of wiring is located it should be closely examined so that the exact cause of failure can be ascertained. A short circuit can often be detected by shaking the wire and listening carefully. As it contacts metal, the characteristic crackling of current short-circuiting can

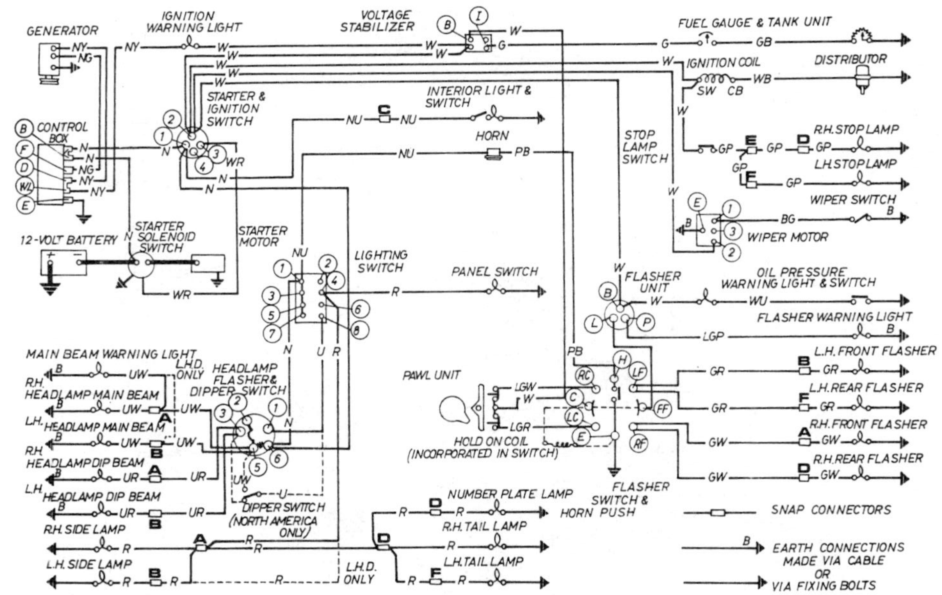

FIG. 7. WIRING DIAGRAM FOR THE HILLMAN IMP

Examine this diagram when checking electrical faults on a Hillman Imp or Super Imp.

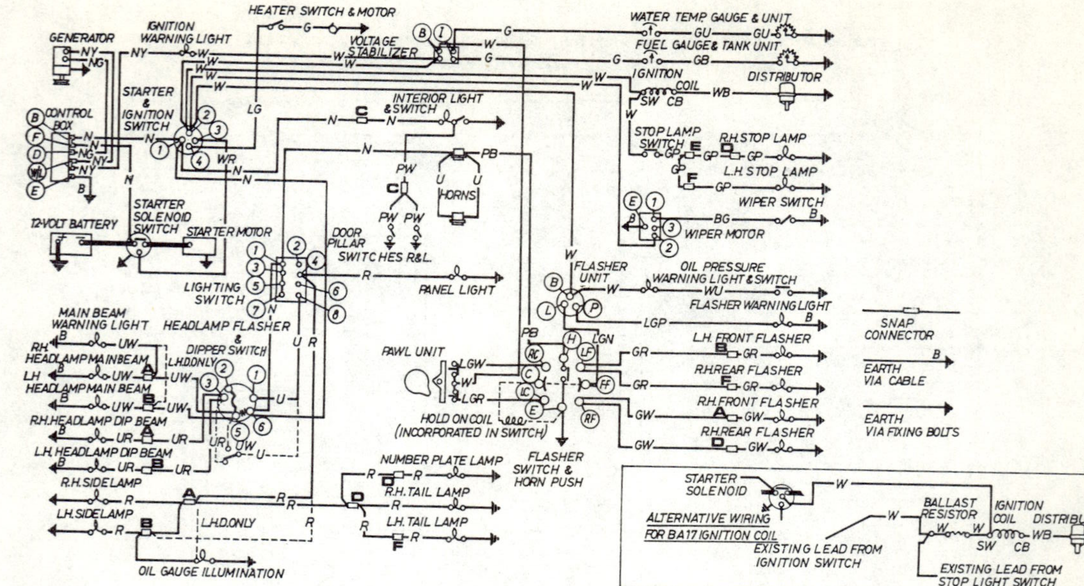

FIG. 8. WIRING DIAGRAM FOR THE SINGER CHAMOIS

KEY TO CABLE SLEEVE COLOURS (FIGS. 7 AND 8)

B.	Black	N.	Brown	U.	Blue
G.	Green	P.	Purple	W.	White
LG.	Light green	R.	Red	Y.	Yellow

easily be heard. A break in the wire, concealed by the outer insulation, can usually be found by holding each end and pulling gently. If the inner cable has broken the lead will stretch at the point of the break.

Where the suspect lead is a very long one and is inaccessible, an alternative method of checking is to by-pass it with a temporary external lead. This is connected to the terminal at each end, and the switch is then operated. If the hitherto inoperative component—a tail light, for instance —works when thus connected it shows that the fault is in the lead. In some cases it is possible to draw a new lead through a conduit by using the old lead as a guide. The new lead is securely fastened to the old one by wiring the terminals together, for example. The old lead is then withdrawn, pulling the new lead into position.

When repairing fractured leads it is important to ensure that no undue electrical stresses are set up and that the insulation is made good. All joints should be twisted together neatly, and well wound with insulating tape to make leakage impossible. Where terminals have been undone they must be done up again tightly, since a loose terminal can cause electrical stresses through spasmodic breaking of the circuit. Where a soldered joint has failed it is essential that it be remade with solder, and not merely retaped.

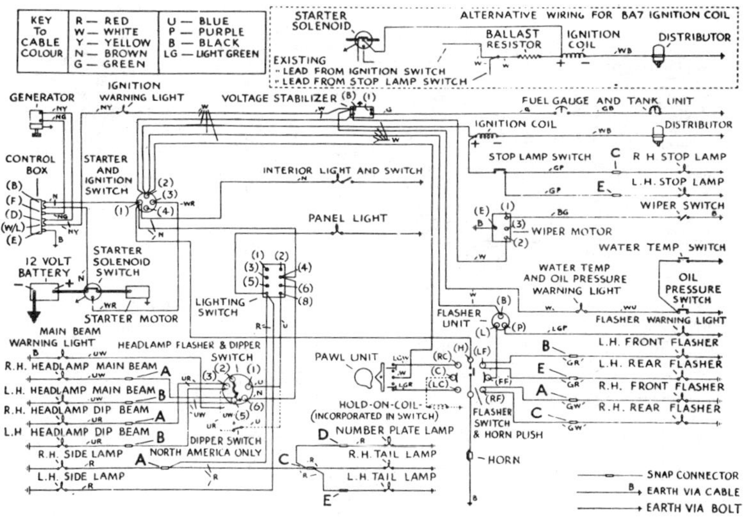

Fig. 9. Wiring Diagram for the Imp de Luxe Mk. 2

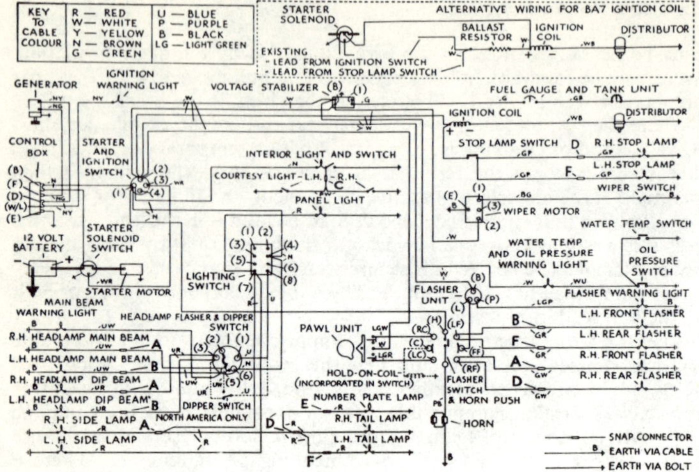

FIG. 10. WIRING DIAGRAM FOR THE IMP SUPER MK. 2

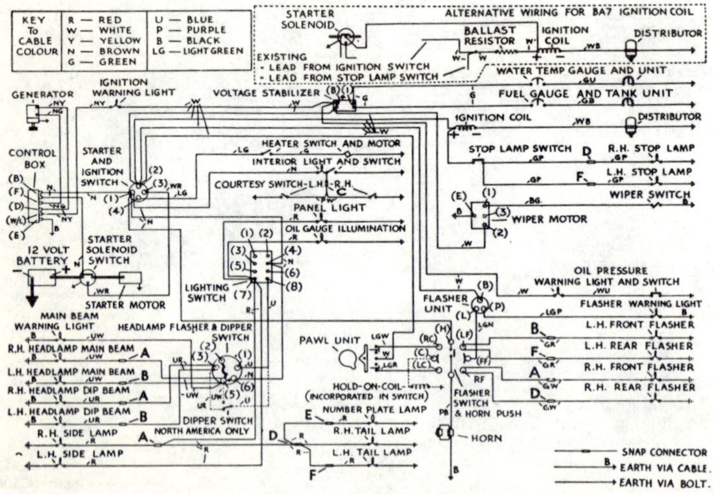

FIG. 11. WIRING DIAGRAM FOR THE SINGER CHAMOIS MK. 2

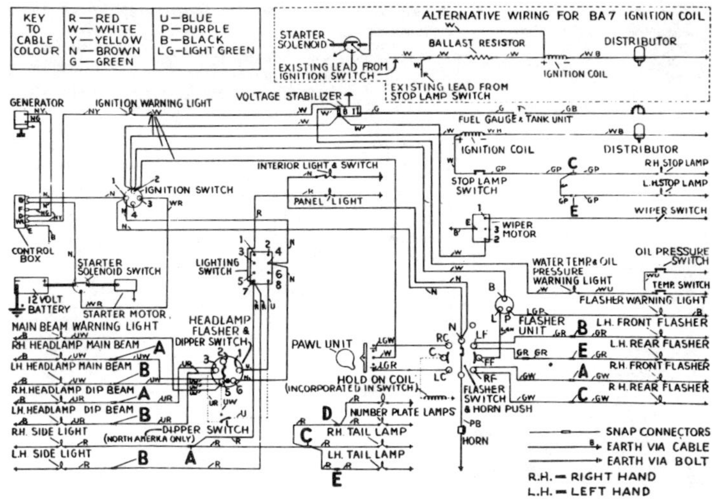

FIG. 12. WIRING DIAGRAM FOR THE IMP VAN AND HILLMAN HUSKY ESTATE

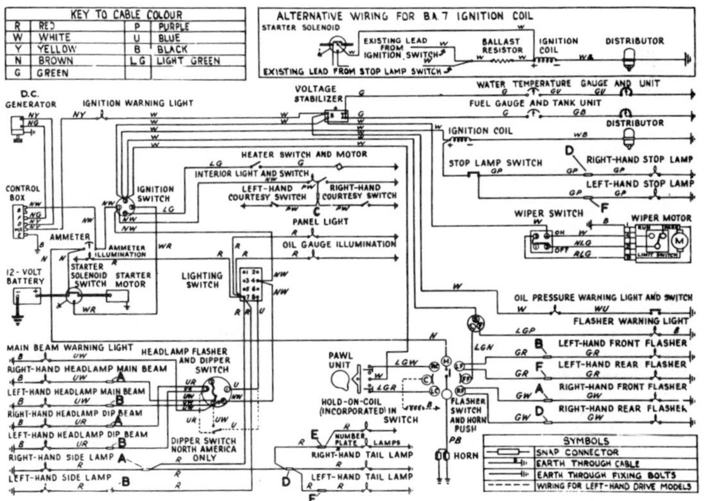

FIG. 13. WIRING DIAGRAM FOR THE IMP SPORT AND CHAMOIS SPORT

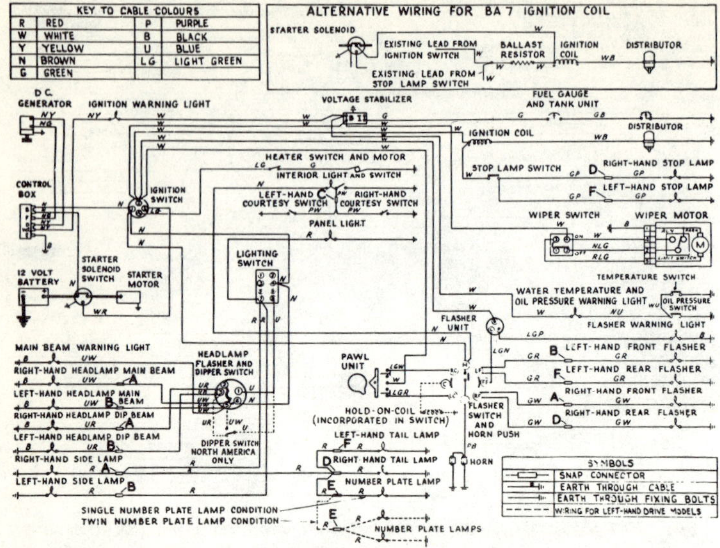

FIG. 14. WIRING DIAGRAM FOR THE IMP CALIFORNIAN COUPÉ

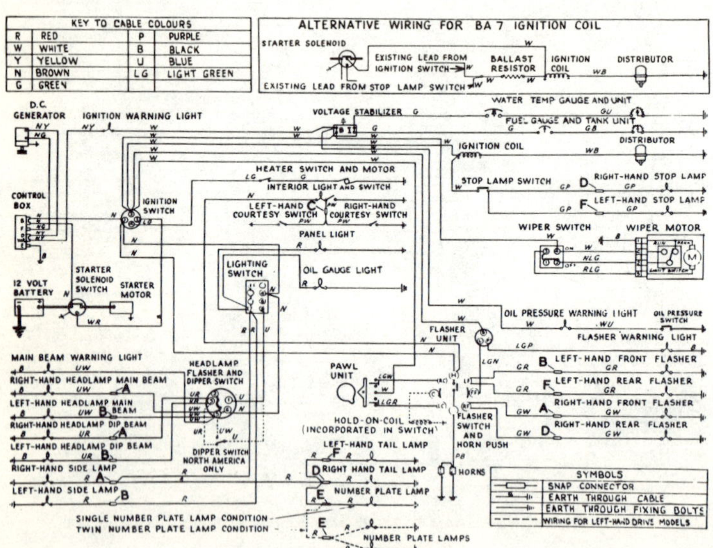

FIG. 15. WIRING DIAGRAM FOR THE SINGER CHAMOIS COUPÉ

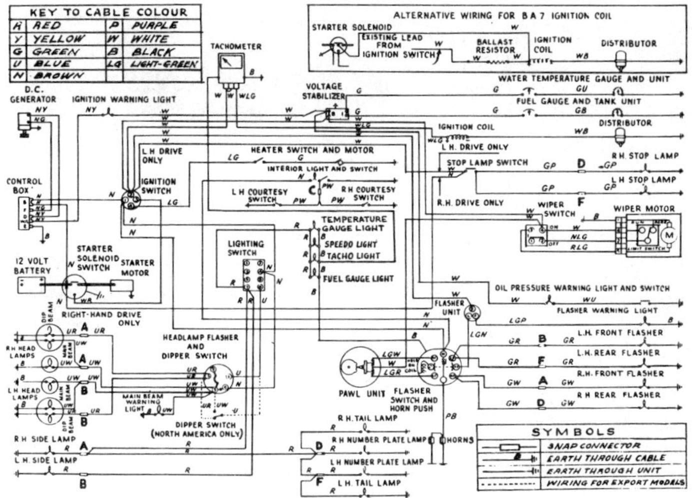

FIG. 16. WIRING DIAGRAM FOR THE SUNBEAM STILETTO COUPÉ

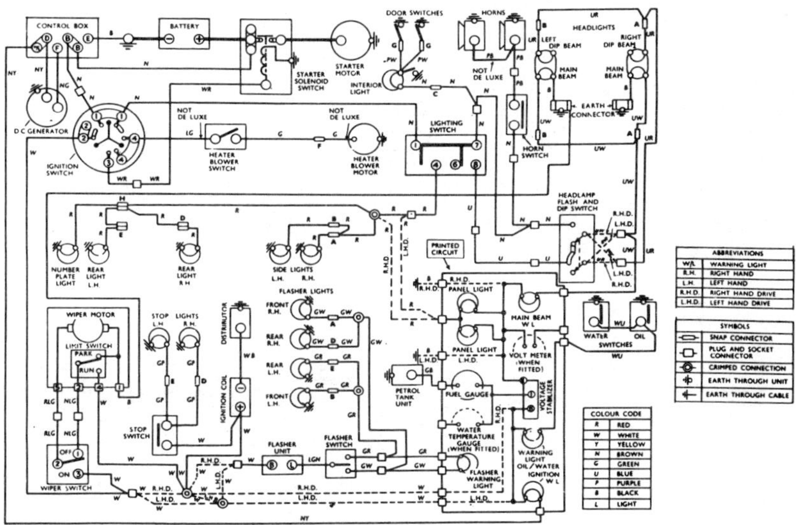

FIG. 17. WIRING DIAGRAM FOR THE IMP DE LUXE, IMP SUPER AND IMP CALIFORNIAN

This diagram applies to cars from Chassis No. B.413000001 (de luxe); 443000001 (Super); and B.402000001 (California).

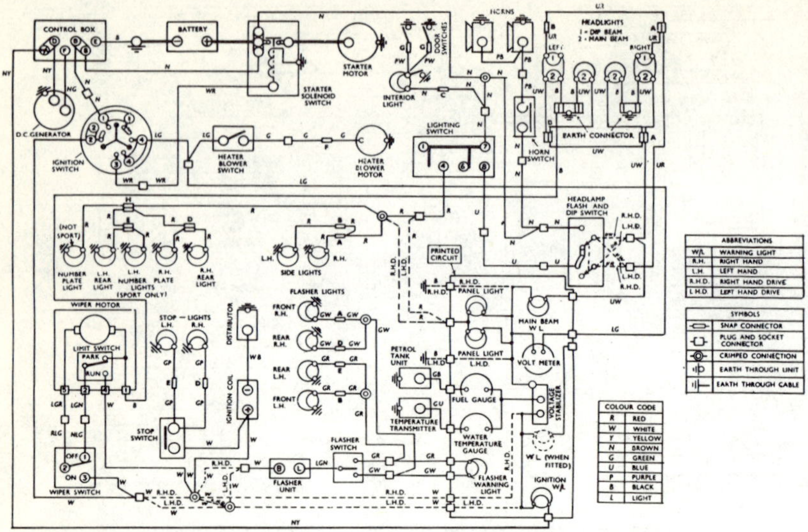

FIG. 18. WIRING DIAGRAM FOR THE SINGER CHAMOIS SALOON, COUPÉ,
AND SPORT

This diagram applies to cars from Chassis Nos. B.733000001 (Saloon); B.722000001 (Coupé);
and B.793000001 (Sport).

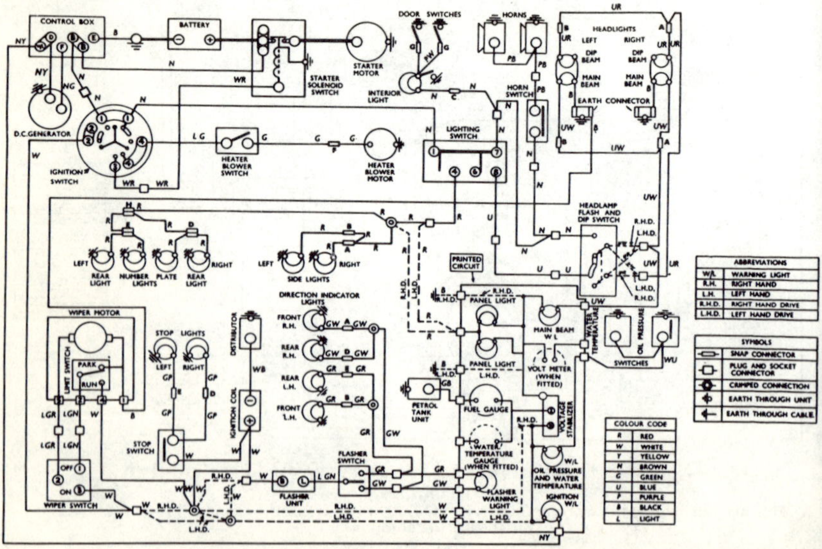

FIG. 19. WIRING DIAGRAM FOR IMP SPORT

This diagram applies to cars from Chassis No. B.493000001.

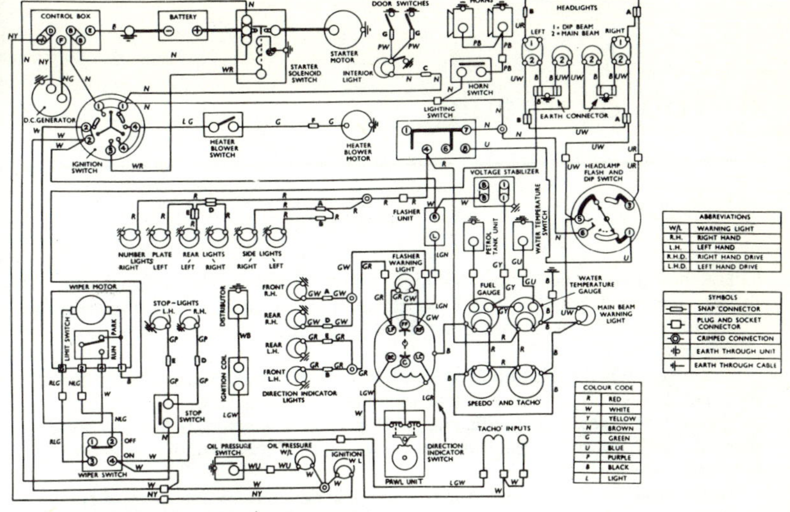

FIG. 20. WIRING DIAGRAM FOR THE SUNBEAM STILETTO
This diagram applies to cars from Chassis No. B.302000001.

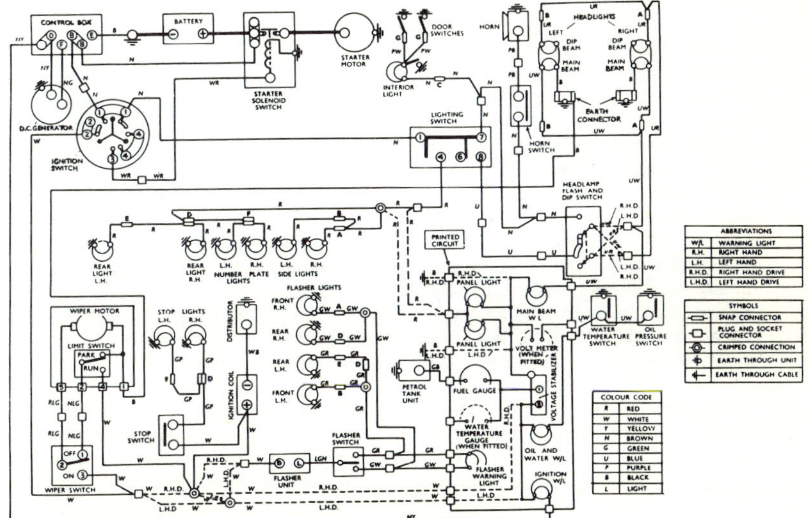

FIG. 21. WIRING DIAGRAM FOR IMP VAN AND HUSKY ESTATE
This diagram applies to cars from Chassis No. B.463000001 (vans) and B.482000001 (Estate).

4 Top overhauls

THERE has always been an obsession about decarbonizing (commonly called "decoking") which has been elevated to the status of a universal "cure all" for any ills which beset a petrol engine. In fact, it is nothing of the sort.

Years ago, when fuels and oils were less scientifically developed a rather frequent "decoke" or top overhaul *was* vital if the engine was to continue to work with reasonable efficiency. If it was neglected heavy carbon deposits built up on the pistons and valves, and in the combustion chambers and cylinder ports.

Today, thanks to the constant research carried out by the oil and fuel companies, internal fouling has been so reduced that it is no longer necessary to decarbonize an engine frequently. Engines have run quite satisfactorily for extremely long periods without having their cylinder heads removed, and on eventual examination carbon deposits were found to be still only moderate.

When Is a Top Overhaul Necessary? One should not, of course, go to extremes when using one's own car for everyday purposes but it is *never* advisable to disturb a mechanism which is running well. The primary purpose today of a top overhaul is to check the valves and their clearances and grind-in the valves on their seats in the cylinder head. This should be done for the first time after covering 10,000–15,000 miles and then at 40,000 mile intervals, the mileage between later top overhauls being determined mainly by cylinder compression tests. With its 10 to 1 compression ratio the Imp should give cylinder pressure readings of 185–200 lb per sq in. on a garage's compression tester. Owing to individual variations, not every cylinder will return exactly this figure, but if there is any significant variation on even *one* cylinder (more than 10 lb per sq in. difference between them) the time has come to remove the cylinder head and to examine the state of the valves, grind them in, and decarbonize.

Items Required. Before doing any actual work, obtain a "decoke" set from a Chrysler dealer. This will contain all the gaskets and seals which are needed. I always fit new valve springs during a top overhaul. They are quite cheap, and when the engine is stripped one might just as well take the chance of practising a bit of preventive replacement and so ensure that the engine will give of its best from the start until the next top overhaul is due.

Besides having the necessary spares available it is also essential to have the torque spanner and socket spanners recommended on page 12; a thin-walled box spanner to fit the camshaft cover nuts ($\frac{7}{16}$ in. A/F); a small weight on a 3 in. length of wire; a screwdriver with square blade 18 in. long (or the special Chrysler camshaft-chain tensioner, Part No. RG 354); some stout cardboard or clean newspaper; a scraper for removing carbon deposits, a valve spring compressor, a suction-type valve grinding tool; a wire brush; a hammer and drift; several screwdrivers; and a set of open-ended and ring spanners.

First Clean the Engine. Start by cleaning the engine thoroughly. A clean engine is far more pleasant to work on, and there is less chance of dirt getting into its internals. An Imp engine compartment unfortunately tends to become fouled very quickly and therefore this preliminary cleaning is very important.

The best method of cleaning is to brush grease solvent over the entire engine compartment and, after allowing a few minutes for it to soak in, to hose it off with a *gentle* flow from a suitable hose. Do not direct the flow against any part of the electrical system. Then mop up with some rag or, better still, clean the power unit the night before so that it has twelve hours in which to drain before you start work.

DISMANTLING PROCEDURE

The following is the correct dismantling procedure for undertaking a top overhaul—

1. Remove the Air Filter. Begin by detaching the battery earth lead. Then with a screwdriver loosen the wire clip which secures the air filter body to the carburettor. It should be free enough to move easily, but you need not detach the clamping screw completely. A few turns with the screwdriver is quite sufficient.

Next remove the single nut and bolt which hold the air filter body to the lug on the inlet manifold just forward of the fuel pump. The filter is now free from the engine, but to remove it from the engine compartment its upper body must be separated from the lower one. Do this by lifting the entire filter from the carburettor and edging it into the space in front of the latter, i.e. *towards the front* of the car. This allows you to drop it down and so reach the wing nut on top of the filter body; this is almost inaccessible when the filter is in its normal position. Undo the wing nut and separate the upper body from the lower one (*see* also Fig. 22). Lift out the upper body, leaving the lower body wedged in the engine compartment where it can remain until removal of the cylinder head makes it easier to lift out.

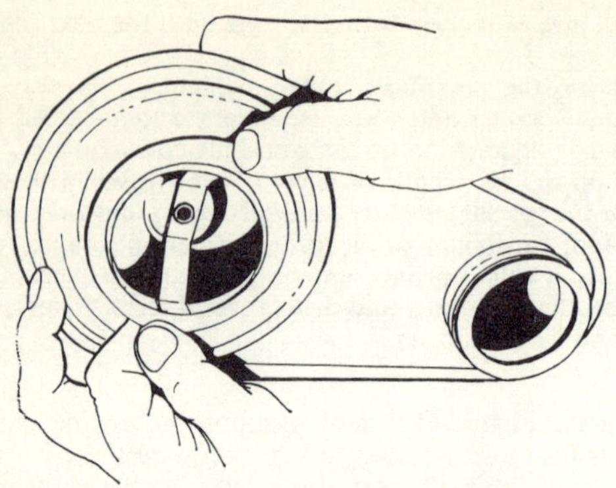

Fig. 22. The Air Cleaner Ring

To ensure that the air is properly filtered, it is essential that this rubber ring is correctly seated when the filter top is replaced.

Fig. 23. The Fuel Pump Gaskets

Do not damage or lose these packings when removing the fuel pump. As is explained here they have two vital jobs to do, and the same number and size of shims must be fitted here if the pump is to operate. Only one gasket is shown removed.

2. Remove the Fuel Pump. Chrysler recommend that the fuel pump should be removed and tied out of harm's way somewhere in the engine compartment with the lead from the fuel tank still attached.

This is a simple job, entailing the release of the feed line to the carburettor (a push fit on the pump) and freeing the two $\frac{1}{2}$ in. A/F nuts which hold the pump to its studs. It can then be lifted off. Note, however, that the gaskets (*see* Fig. 23) which are interposed between the pump and the cam cover determine what pressure of fuel the pump will deliver to the carburettor. Do not lose or damage any of them, and ensure that they are properly refitted when rebuilding the unit.

Some mechanics prefer to leave the pump in place and merely detach the fuel lines instead. When doing this it is advisable to plug the main fuel feed from the petrol tank.

3. Remove the Cam Cover. Before loosening the cam-cover nuts place a drip-tray under the engine beneath the manifolds. This is to catch the oil which is trapped in the cover, because of the inclination of the engine. Some mechanics minimize this oil loss by jacking up the front of the car for a few minutes before starting work, so allowing the oil to drain back into the sump through the camshaft tunnel.

When the drip-tray is in position remove the eight $\frac{7}{16}$ in. A/F nuts and their washers which secure the cam cover. Here the thin-walled box spanner is a vital tool. Most ring and socket spanners will be too thick to engage the nuts in the shallow recesses cast in the cover, and if your Imp is secondhand you may well find that a previous owner has left them little more than fingertight for that very reason. With the nuts off, lift the cam cover. The gasket will tend to stick and may tear, but as a new gasket must always be used whenever the cam cover is detached, this point is of no practical importance.

4. Check the Valve Clearances. Now comes the point at which the recommended procedure for the Imp varies from that of most other light cars. The valve clearances must be measured so that one can decide what treatment each valve demands. If clearances are too large, a different shim will be needed between the valve and the tappet block on reassembly. Where the clearance is too small, and the thinnest shim is already in use, a new guide will be needed.

In practice this operation should only be necessary on a second-hand Imp where the condition of the valve seats and faces will not be known, or on a car which one knows has covered far more than the normal mileage between valve grinding. In either of these cases both the valves and their seats will need refacing, rather than grinding-in, and the initial clearance check is then valuable. Where the car's probable condition is known it can be dispensed with, because little metal is removed in a straightforward valve-grinding operation. But even here the valve clearances should be checked *before* the cylinder head is replaced on the engine.

Valve clearances are measured between the back of each cam and the flat face of the tappet block, with the peak of the cam pointing towards the valve-cover centre. Start with No. 1 cam and work as tabulated below in that order. Rotate the engine until the valve is fully open.

PROCEDURE FOR CHECKING VALVE CLEARANCES

Valve fully open	Measure clearance on
No. 4 cyl. exhaust valve	No. 1 cyl. exhaust valve
No. 3 cyl. inlet valve	No. 2 cyl. inlet valve
No. 2 cyl. exhaust valve	No. 3 cyl. exhaust valve
No. 4 cyl. inlet valve	No. 1 cyl. inlet valve
No. 1 cyl. exhaust valve	No. 4 cyl. exhaust valve
No. 2 cyl. inlet valve	No. 3 cyl. inlet valve
No. 3 cyl. exhaust valve	No. 2 cyl. exhaust valve
No. 1 cyl. inlet valve	No. 4 cyl. inlet valve

The engine can be turned either by fitting a spanner on the crankshaft pulley bolt-head, or by using a spanner on the water-pump pulley nut, while tensioning the longest run of the drive belt (the lower one) either with one's hand or, better still, with a smooth and blunt piece of wood.

The valve clearances, measured with feeler gauges, should be 0·004–0·006 in. for inlet valves, and 0·006–0·008 in. for exhaust valves with engine cold.

5. Remove the Camshaft. With a punch bend back the locking tab of the camshaft's fixing bolt. Now insert a long-handled screwdriver or the chain-tensioning tool into the camshaft tunnel alongside the upper run of the chain, and block up the rest of the tunnel mouth either with lintless rag or with clean newspaper.

Using a $\frac{9}{16}$ in. A/F spanner, remove the centre bolt from the sprocket and take away the tab-washer and the plain washer (*see* Fig. 24). Here there is a danger that the small dowel which locates the sprocket will fall out and enter the camshaft tunnel. Prevent this by keeping one finger on it while, with the other hand, pressing the chain tensioner away from the chain with the screwdriver shaft. It will then be possible to ease the sprocket downwards, out of the chain. When this has been done, withdraw the camshaft driving peg (*see* Fig. 25).

Keeping the camshaft-drive chain tensioned with one hand, so that it does not free itself from the sprocket on the crankshaft, affix the weight to it by means of the length of wire and allow it to hang down from the

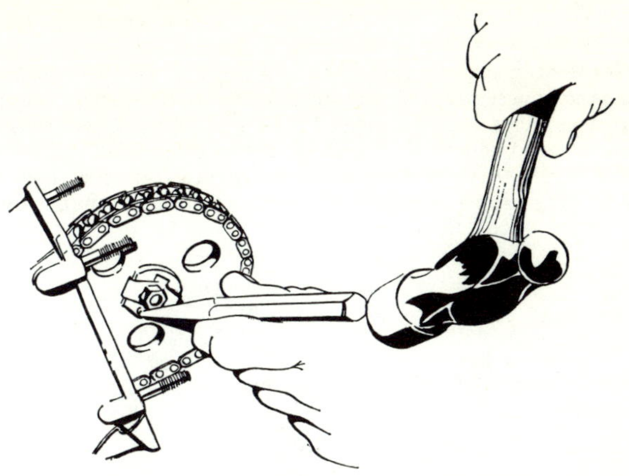

FIG. 24. TAB-WASHER FOR CAMSHAFT SPROCKET

When freeing the camshaft sprocket, first flatten the tab-washer shown above.

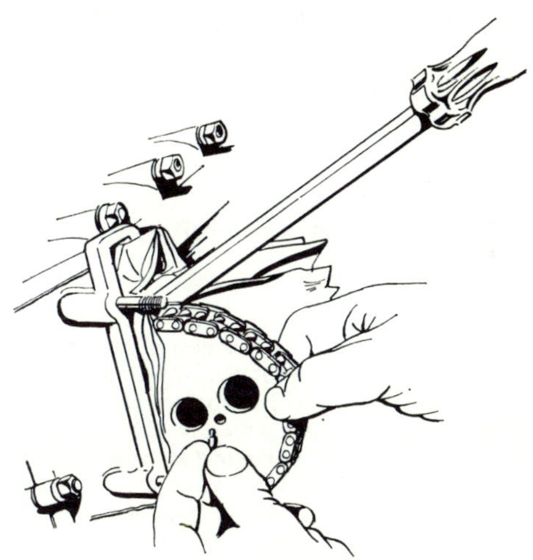

FIG. 25. REMOVING DRIVING PEG ON CAMSHAFT

Remove the camshaft set-screw, the tab-washer, and the distance piece. Then carefully lift out the driving peg. If it is tight it could be left in position until the sprocket has been removed from the camshaft flange.

tunnel for the camshaft driving chain (*see* Fig. 26). Strictly speaking, this is perhaps an unnecessary precaution because even if the chain does happen to disengage, it can easily be juggled back into place, if necessary using a long wire hook to help to get it back on the sprocket teeth.

With a punch, mark the camshaft bearing-caps so that they will be refitted in their proper positions. Then release the cap nuts slowly and

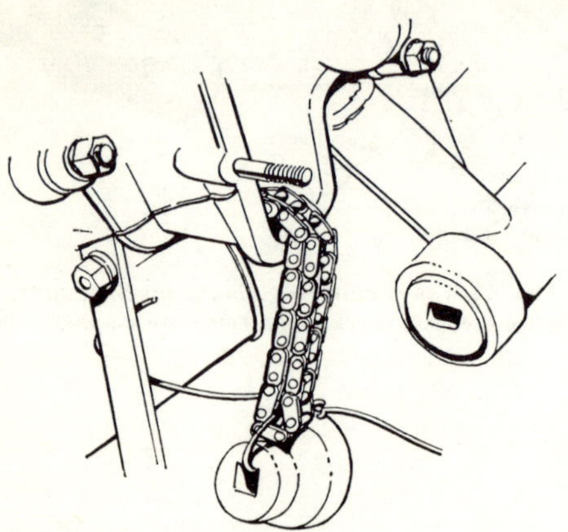

FIG. 26. THE CAMSHAFT DRIVE CHAIN

Tie a weight on the camshaft drive chain so that it hangs down as shown during dismantling.

evenly until the caps can be lifted away. Be careful not to let the bearing shells fall out when you do so. The camshaft is now free and should be removed from the engine.

6. Remove the Tappet-block Housing. The barrel-shaped tappet blocks must be lifted from their housing. This is best done with the suction cap from the end of a valve grinding tool; it can be pressed on the face of each tappet block. Owing to oil drag it is probable that at least some of the valve-adjusting shims will be lifted with the tappet blocks. Therefore check inside each tappet block immediately it is taken out to see if its shim is adhering to its inner face. If it is, separate them and mark both the shim and the tappet block so that it will be possible to refit them in their original positions.

When marking each shim and tappet block do *not* scratch their operating or bearing surfaces. It is best to mark them by wiping them free of oil and applying to each a small piece of adhesive plastic tape on which their cylinder number and valve numbers can be written; for example: No. 4

(ex); No. 1 (in). After all eight tappet blocks have been removed take off the eight $\frac{7}{16}$ in. A/F nuts securing the tappet-block housing and slide it off its studs (*see* Fig. 27).

7. Remove the Cylinder Head. Before removing the cylinder head it is obviously necessary to drain the cooling system. Remove the radiator filler cap to prevent air locks, and open the two drain taps. One is situated on the radiator and the other on the right-hand side of the cylinder block.

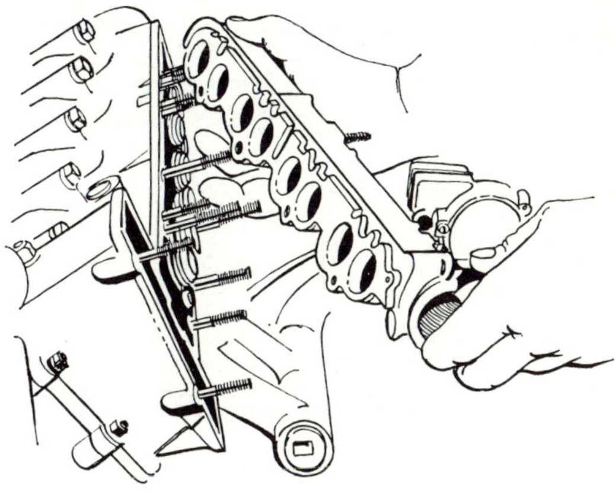

FIG. 27. TAPPET-BLOCK HOUSING REMOVAL

Before lifting off the tappet-block housing, the camshaft and all the tappet blocks must be detached. Do not lose the shims between the valve stems and the tappet blocks, or mix them up.

Where the coolant contains an anti-freeze mixture, this can be saved by allowing the coolant to drain into a clean bowl for subsequent use when the top overhaul is completed.

Next remove the silencer by freeing its clamp on the exhaust manifold and releasing the centre nut which secures it to the support bracket. Remove the ten $\frac{9}{16}$ in. A/F bolts located around the cylinder head and the two $\frac{9}{16}$ in. A/F nuts on the camshaft-chain tunnel shown at *A* and *B* in Fig. 28. Loosen each nut a little at a time, working in the sequence shown in Fig. 28 so as to avoid distortion. The light-alloy cylinder head is then free to be removed, save on twin-Stromberg models, where an oil drain pipe to the block is fitted.

Before lifting the cylinder head off, however, disconnect the carburettor's throttle control linkage and then, supporting the camshaft chain by hand, temporarily release the weight which has been holding it. Now lift off the cylinder head, feeding the camshaft chain through the chain tunnel, and when it is clear of the car, lay it carefully down on a bench or table. Remember that, being made of light alloy, its machined surfaces are very vulnerable to scratching and damage.

Replace the weight on the chain and allow it to hang down again. Then remove the old cylinder-head gasket which must *not* be used again and

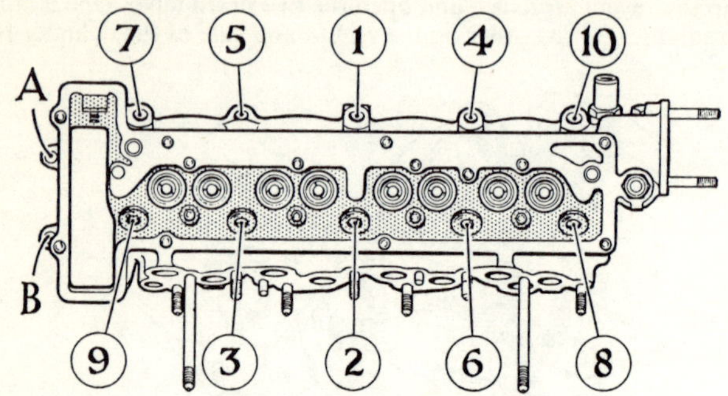

FIG. 28. THE CORRECT SEQUENCE FOR LOOSENING AND TIGHTENING THE
CYLINDER-HEAD BOLTS

As it is made of light alloy, the Imp cylinder head is particularly vulnerable to distortion
if its ten securing bolts are not tightened or loosened in the sequence shown above.

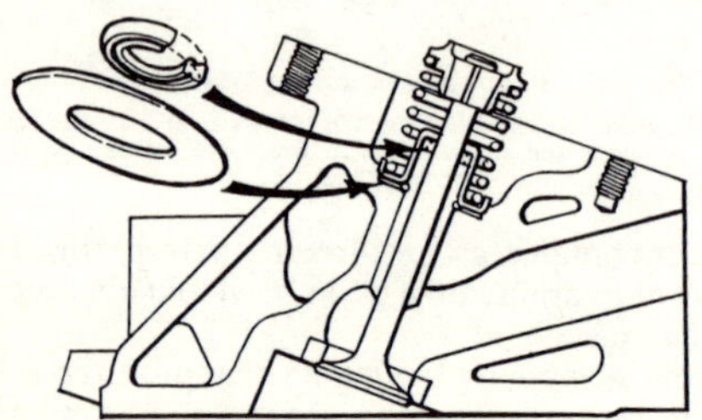

FIG. 29. OIL SEALS FOR INLET VALVES

Each inlet valve has two oil seals, and they are located (as shown by the arrows) under the
bottom valve-spring collars. Do not mix them up and do not fit them to any exhaust
valves.

also take off the small rubber joint-ring which you will find in the top rear corner of the cylinder-block face. This seals the oilway to the valve gear and it is essential that when reassembly is undertaken this ring is fitted. Chrysler suggest that it should be tightly tied to one of the cylinder-head studs so that there will be no danger of its being overlooked.

8. Remove the Valves. Detach the manifolds, held by eight nuts, and also the two locating pegs, and then use a valve-spring compressor to free the eight valves whose springs are held by split collets. If the steel collars, on which the lower ends of the valve springs rest, are removed note that the *inlet* valve-springs' collars have rubber sealing rings interposed between each collar and the top of the valve guide, and joint washers are provided under the collar faces (*see* Fig. 29). These are fitted to prevent oil being drawn into the valve guides and so entering the combustion chambers. They are not fitted to the collars for the exhaust-valve springs, nor when dual valve springs are used.

Sparking Plugs and Vacuum Pipe. Detach the plug caps and unscrew the four sparking plugs, subsequently detaching the rubber dust covers. Pull the vacuum pipe off the carburettor, where it is attached by a rubber connector, and detach its clip from the cam cover.

VALVE GRINDING AND DECARBONIZING

Decarbonizing the Combustion Chambers. When doing this, chip off all carbon deposits with a stick of solder or a piece of hardwood sharpened to a wedge shape. Alternatively use a good proprietary scraper. Be careful not to damage or scratch the light-alloy metal surface. While decarbonizing each combustion chamber it pays to re-insert both valves to prevent the valve seats becoming damaged during the removal of carbon deposits. If you use a wire brush, take special care.

Grinding-in the Valves. Clean the cylinder-head ports thoroughly and then attend to the valves. All carbon deposits should be removed from their heads before grinding-in is commenced. Do this in the usual manner. Smear a little *coarse* grinding paste around the face of each valve in turn (assuming that the valve face and valve seat are considerably pitted; if not, use fine paste), and then place the valve on its seat in the cylinder head.

Press the suction-type valve grinding tool against the valve head and oscillate the valve by rubbing the tool between your hands. After about a dozen oscillations lift the tool, complete with valve, and turn it through 45 degrees. Then press the valve firmly against its seat again and proceed as before. This sequence and procedure should be continued until an examination of the valve and its seat show that on each there is an unbroken thin grey line of contact right round. Then remove the coarse grinding-in paste with a paraffin-damped rag and smear the valve face with some fine grinding-in paste. Replace the valve on its seat and continue grinding-in until a fine silver-grey continuous contact line is obtained on the valve face and valve seat. There should be no pitting visible. Excessive grinding-in, however, should be avoided, otherwise the valves may become "pocketed." Where a valve face is extensively and deeply pitted it is necessary to have the valve refaced. The same applies to the valve seat.

This is an expert's job which should be done at a well equipped garage service station.

When all valves have been ground in, the cylinder-head should be well washed in petrol to clear away any remaining traces of abrasive grinding paste. The valves can then be refitted—using new oil seals and joints on the inlet-valve collar, and new springs with the help of the valve spring compressor.

Decarbonizing the Pistons. This job should next be attended to. To avoid disturbing the oil-sealing properties of a worn engine, it is usual to leave in position a ring of carbon about $\frac{1}{8}$ in. wide round the circumference of each piston. If you have an old piston ring which you can slip into the

FIG. 30. TURNING THE CRANKSHAFT WHEN DECARBONIZING
To bring a different piston to T.D.C. for decarbonizing, press and move the fan belt while maintaining tension on the camshaft-drive chain.

cylinder bore above the piston crown, you will find that it makes an excellent "mask" for protecting this carbon ring.

While keeping tension on the timing chain with one hand, turn the engine over by means of the fan driving belt (*see* Fig. 30) with the other hand to bring each piston in turn to the top of its stroke. Block off the chain tunnel with rag or newspaper so that no carbon dust can find its way into the oil sump, and from rolled newspaper make up small shields which can be slipped into the water jacket at the lower edge of each cylinder. This will catch carbon chippings which would otherwise fall into the water passages. Decarbonize the crown of each piston thoroughly, being careful not to scratch its soft surface, and remove all carbon chippings and dust. None of this must be allowed to get between the pistons and cylinder bores. This is another good reason for using an old piston ring as a mask.

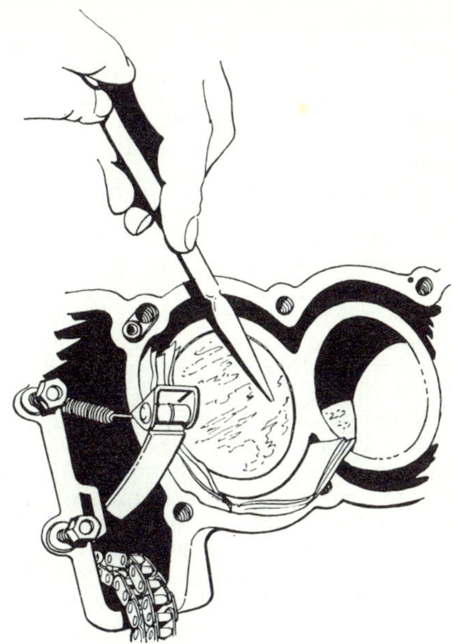

FIG. 31. DECARBONIZING A PISTON

When scraping carbon from the piston crowns it is advisable to protect the water jackets by inserting strips of folded newspaper which prevent chippings entering. Scrape the piston crowns absolutely clean. It is good practice to leave a ring of carbon around the circumference of the piston so as to act as an oil seal, particularly in the case of an engine which has done a very considerable mileage.

REASSEMBLING THE ENGINE

Start assembly work by replacing the tappet-block housing, the tappet shims, the tappet blocks, and finally the camshaft. This must be properly tightened down with a tension of 6 lb ft on the bearing-cap nuts.

The Valve Clearances. Now check the valve clearances again, temporarily refitting the camshaft-drive sprocket so that the camshaft can be turned by hand into the correct position. From the data which you obtain you should calculate whether a different shim is needed and, if so, which one it is.

Assume that the feeler gauge reading is such that the gap is obviously too small. The recommended "average" gap for an inlet valve is 0·005 in. (i.e. 0·004 in. + 0·006 in. divided by 2). If the feeler gauge which will just fit is 0·003 in., the shim needed is one which is 0·005 in. minus 0·003 in. thinner—i.e. a shim 0·002 in. thinner than the existing one. If, on the other hand, the gap is too great, the difference between the actual reading and the recommended "average" has to be added to the shim.

Valve-clearance shims are available in a range of sizes from 0·087 in. to 0·111 in., increasing by 0·001 in. stages, so that accurate adjustment is normally possible. Where even this shim range is not adequate, up to 0·030 in. may be ground off the end of the valve stem to obtain the correct clearance. The "average" is 0·007 in. for an exhaust valve.

Replacing the Cylinder Head. The tappet blocks should now be removed. The new cylinder-head gasket and the rubber sealing ring should then be positioned on the cylinder block, the weight removed from the camshaft-drive chain, and the crankshaft turned so that all the pistons are halfway down their cylinder bores. This is vital, otherwise the valves may foul them later. Because the face of the cylinder block is at a pronounced angle and the gasket may tend to slip away from it Chrysler suggest that a dummy cylinder-head stud be made up. This is simply a stud with a screwdriver slot cut in it which can be inserted into one of the cylinder-head bolt holes to locate the gasket while the cylinder-head is being offered up. Afterwards, when one or two cylinder-head bolts have been inserted, simply unscrew the dummy stud.

The above tip certainly saves a certain amount of fiddling because, as the cylinder-head gasket must be fitted dry, there is no other means of keeping it in place while the cylinder-head is being eased into position in the rather confined space available.

After replacing the manifolds, using new gaskets, and after torqueing the nuts to 6 lb ft, lift the cylinder head into place. Do not forget that the camshaft-drive chain has to be fed through the tunnel as you do this. It helps if you have an assistant at this stage, though it can be done single-handed by resting the front of the cylinder head on the cylinder block and supporting it with one hand while the other deals with the camshaft-drive chain.

Now tighten all the ten cylinder-head bolts finger-tight. Afterwards torque them in the correct sequence (*see* Fig. 28) to 36 lb ft. Then tighten the two camshaft-drive tunnel nuts shown at *A* and *B* to 15 lb ft.

Refit the tappet-block housing, tightening the securing nuts to 6 lb ft; place the valve-clearance adjusting shims in their recesses in the valve collars; lightly oil each tappet block and insert it correctly in the tappet-block housing.

Fitting the Camshaft. Now position the camshaft in its three bearings and fit the bearing caps. Make sure that they are replaced in their original positions. Tighten the cap-securing nuts with your fingers and then torque them to 6 lb ft. As the nuts are tightened, the camshaft will be pulled down against the resistance of the valve springs. No set tightening procedure is suggested by the manufacturers, but I prefer to deal with the centre cap first; then the front one; and finally the rear one.

The manufacturers suggest that at this stage the valve clearances again be checked (an easy job, provided the camshaft sprocket is loosely fitted so that the camshaft can be turned), but most Imp private owners will probably choose to omit it. In nine cases out of ten they will be justified; but bear in mind that *if* the clearances have in fact altered during engine assembly, to check and rectify them *after* the engine has been completely assembled is a long and time-wasting job. At this stage it can be done quickly. The procedure is exactly the same as that mentioned on page 31.

Retiming the Camshaft. Very carefully turn the engine over to bring No. 1 piston (the one nearest the back of the car) to T.D.C. Do this by rotating the camshaft until the slot in the belt pulley lines up with the pointer above it, and the rotor of the distributor points to No. 1 sparking plug lead-position in its cap.

To do the above you will probably have to remove the camshaft, because it will hold some of the valves open and these will foul the pistons. It may be possible to avoid this by judicious manipulation of the camshaft, or merely by slackening off its bearing-cap nuts sufficiently to allow all eight valves to close. But camshaft removal is safest, and it makes the next job easier.

Position the camshaft so that the peaks of No. 1 cylinder's two cams are *at the same height* above the cylinder-head face. Then refit the bearing caps and torque the nuts to 6 lb ft.

Refitting the Camshaft Drive. Insert the special service tool, or a long-bladed screwdriver, so that the pressure of the chain tensioner can be relieved. Then release the weight from the chain and spread the chain upwards with your hand so that it is in its working position. Engage the sprocket with it in such a way that the line scribed on the sprocket face is parallel with the top edge of the camshaft-drive tunnel (*see* Fig. 32). Press the small dowel into position in the sprocket, and ease the sprocket over its boss and into position on the camshaft.

Fit the sprocket securing-bolt and washers. Fit a new tab-washer (*see* Fig. 25) on the bolt first, followed by the thick plain washer. Then screw home the centre bolt, torqued to 19 lb ft, and turn one edge of the tab-washer over the hexagon to secure the centre bolt.

Final Engine Assembly. The remainder of the assembly work is straight-forward. Replace the valve gear cover, using a new gasket, and tighten its nuts to 6 lb ft. Secure the silencer clamp and support straps; replace the carburettor linkage; bolt the fuel pump back on the camshaft cover (6 lb ft torque); connect the fuel lines; replace the water hoses; reconnect the vacuum pipe; fit the air filter after renewing its element (*see* page 29).

Clean and if necessary regap the sparking plugs or, better still, fit new plugs after gapping their electrodes to 0·025 in. Also reconnect the distributor leads to the four sparking plugs in the correct order. Finally,

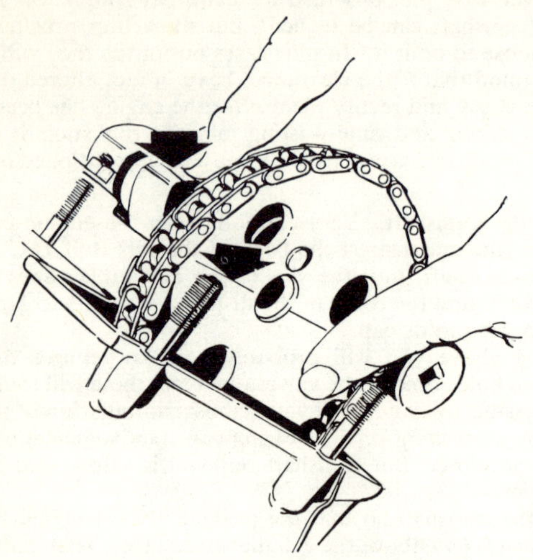

Fig. 32. Setting the Valve Timing

When replacing the camshaft-drive sprocket, No. 1 cam (the rear one) must be set in the position shown above, with the scribed line on the sprocket (indicated here by a large arrow) parallel with the top edge of the camshaft-chain tunnel.

reconnect the battery and fill the cooling system with water. In winter, add Bluecol AA anti-freeze, which is specially compounded to prevent corrosion in light-alloy water jackets.

When the assembly of the engine is completed it may prove necessary to "bleed" the heater system. The need for doing this is shown by reduced heater efficiency, indicating that air has entered the cooling system. The correct "bleeding" procedure is described on page 69 in Chapter 7.

5 Major Overhauls

THERE is a sharp dividing line between overhaul work which can be done by the average private owner with his normal tool kit and that which can be tackled by him only with the help of expensive workshop tools. That line can be drawn forward of the clutch. Complete stripping down and rebuilding the engine is a relatively straightforward business. Renewing the clutch plates demands removal of the engine but is not basically difficult.

Where the transaxle unit (comprising the gearbox and differential) is concerned, the only job which can be done is renewal of the drive-shaft rubber couplings. You can remove the transaxle (an awkward job, but not impossible) and you can take off the selector cover. But beyond this it is special tools all the way. Fourteen are listed and fourteen are needed! Transaxle overhaul is therefore not dealt with here. Figs. 33 and 34 show the major castings and the moving parts of the Imp engine respectively!

Big-end Bearing Renewal. Start by cleaning the engine compartment thoroughly. Then remove the cylinder head as already described, having first drained the sump of oil.

From the bottom of the bell housing remove the gauze flywheel-guard. Remove the 24 sump-securing nuts ($\frac{7}{16}$ in. A/F with spring washers) and the sump can then be withdrawn. Take off the sump-joint gasket and scrap it. A new gasket must *always* be used when replacing the sump.

Check that the connecting-rod big-end bearing caps are *all* clearly marked with their cylinder numbers. These are stamped on the caps on the distributor side of the engine. If you are in any doubt about these numbers, make your own marks so that you can replace the caps in their original positions.

Flatten the tab-washers on the connecting-rod securing bolts and remove the latter. Then take off the lower bearing caps, complete with bearing shells. Push each piston and connecting-rod assembly up through the cylinder and remove it from above.

Detach all worn bearing-shells from the bearing caps and the connecting-rods, and insert new shells. Then offer up each piston and connecting-rod assembly to the cylinder bore, making sure that it goes into its original place. Note also that the word "FRONT" is stamped on the crown of each piston. This indicates the side which must face the crankshaft-pulley end of the engine, i.e. *the rear of the car*.

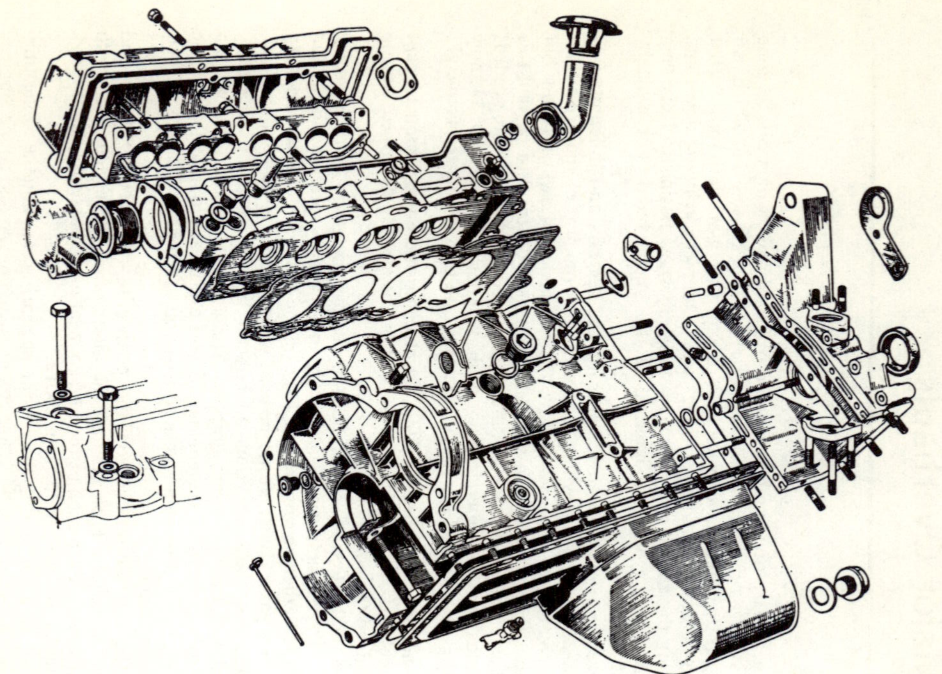

Fig. 33. Imp Engine Castings

This exploded view of the engine castings and their gaskets shows the relationship of the various static parts of the power unit.

Replace the big-end lower bearing-caps with the stamped numbers facing the distributor side, using new tab-washers. Torque the bolts to 18 lb ft and lock them by turning over the tabs on the tab-washers. Grease the new sump-joint gasket and refit the sump. Tighten all nuts finger-tight first, and then torque them to 6 lb ft. That done, rebuild the engine as described later in this chapter, and finally refill the oil sump.

Renewing Small-end Bearing. Up to the stage where the pistons have been removed from the cylinder bores, this is the same procedure as for big-end renewal. Then remove the circlips from the recesses in the

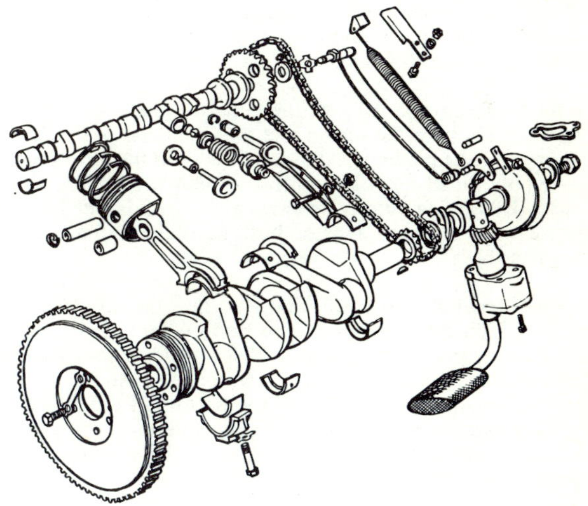

FIG. 34. LAYOUT OF THE VITAL MOVING PARTS OF THE IMP ENGINE

How the moving parts of the engine are related is clearly shown in this drawing of the crankshaft/camshaft and oil pump assembly. The distributor (not shown above) is driven off the upper end of the oil pump shaft.

piston at each end of the gudgeon-pin and scrape off any carbon deposits which have accumulated there.

Warm the piston (the makers recommend that this is done in oil) to 120°F (50°C) and push out the gudgeon-pin. Under no circumstances try to drive out a tight gudgeon-pin from a *cold* piston. This will damage the piston bosses. The gudgeon-pin is a finger push-fit in its piston at 70°F (21°C) room temperature. Under these conditions it is only ust free in the small-end bush.

The small-end bush should be renewed in the normal way. Obtain a bolt which is between three and four times as long as the bush, together with a nut, a couple of very large washers, and a hollow distance piece whose internal bore is slightly greater than the outside diameter of the bush. Place one washer on the bolt and follow this with the distance piece. The washer must bear against the end of this. Insert the free end of the bolt through the bush in the connecting-rod, and at the other side butt the new bush against the old one. Place the second washer on the bolt so that it bears on the end of the new bush, and replace the nut. Make sure that the new bush and the old one are perfectly aligned.

Now tighten the nut slowly, when the new bush will be pressed into the connecting-rod small-end, expelling the old one as it goes in. After fitting, the new bush must be reamed and honed so that the gudgeon-pin is the closest possible fit but is able to turn. A garage or engineering workshop will undertake this part of the work for you.

Fitting the Gudgeon-pin. To refit the gudgeon-pin when rebuilding the engine, again warm both the piston and the small-end of the connecting-rod and then press the pin home. Fit new circlips in the piston bosses, and test the assembly for fit by holding it horizontally and releasing the connecting-rod. It should fall under its own weight. If it is stiff, the gudgeon-pin will have to be removed and the bush eased. Rebuild the engine as previously described.

Piston Ring Renewal. Before fitting new rings the oil glaze should be removed from each cylinder bore. The best method of doing this is to make up a dummy piston from wood. This should fit snugly in the bore with a piece of No. $1\frac{1}{2}$ grade emery cloth wrapped round it.

Using clean non-fluffy rag, mask off the bottom of the cylinder bores. Then insert the dummy piston and work it up and down the bore, turning it as you do so, for three minutes. At the end of this time the walls of the cylinder bore should be criss-crossed with abrasions. Wash down the bore thoroughly with petrol and a clean cloth, and then dry it out. Make quite sure that no abrasive particles find their way into the rest of the engine. Then repeat the process on the other cylinder bores.

The above treatment sounds very drastic. It certainly frightened me! But it is now the normally-recommended Imp procedure because the top ring is chromium-plated; if a new ring reciprocates in a *polished* bore it never beds itself in properly.

Remove the old piston rings and break one of them. Using this as a tool, scrape away all carbon from the piston ring grooves. Then test each new ring in turn in the bore in which it is to go. Position it about an inch down the bore and make sure that it is "square." This can be done by temporarily refitting the piston and placing the ring above it. Then use the piston crown to position the ring accurately.

Check the piston ring gap with a feeler gauge inserted from the top of the cylinder bore. It should fall within the range 0·008–0·013 in. If it is too tight, carefully file one end of the ring with a very fine file to adjust the gap. While doing this, reinsert it in the bore frequently to check progress.

The vertical clearance of the piston ring in its groove must also be correct. When the gap is correct, fit each ring to the piston and measure the groove clearance. This should be 0·0015–0·0035 in. If the ring has less clearance than this, rub one side on emery cloth held on a face plate. A sheet of glass can be used as an alternative.

Fit the rings by springing their ends gently open and easing the rings over the piston. It is usually easier to fit the bottom ring first, bringing it up the piston skirt; followed by the middle ring. The top ring should then be fitted from above the piston crown.

Both the top (chromium-plated) and bottom (oil control) rings can be fitted either way up when new. The second compression ring, however, is stepped and must be fitted with its wider face downwards. This is marked with the word "Bottom." Space the rings so that their gaps are set at equal intervals, i.e. at 120 degrees to each other.

Renewing the Piston. Although it is unlikely that a new piston will be fitted to an existing bore, there is the chance of freak damage which may make this necessary.

Imp pistons come in three diameter grades. To determine which is the appropriate size, the bore in question must be measured with a dial-type measuring gauge to determine its exact diameter. From this, subtract the piston skirt clearance (0·008/0·0014 in.) and use the grade of piston whose diameter comes nearest to this figure. Piston diameters are given in the Appendix on page 117.

Removing the Engine. For work on the crankshaft main bearings, etc., the engine must be removed from the car. To do this, drain the radiator and cylinder block and also the oil from the sump. Detach the battery leads and remove the battery. Where an oil cooler is fitted, undo the unions connecting it to the top of the filter body, and its own securing nuts, and lift it out of place. Then jack up the rear of the car and block it so that you can work underneath it, having chocked the front wheels. Remove all the lower bell-housing nuts except the bottom nut, which should be left finger-tight.

Insert blocks under the transaxle as close to the engine as possible. Then detach the silencer; unbolt the clutch operating cylinder and tie it (still attached to its hydraulic lead) to the bulkhead.

Now block up the engine. A section of railway sleeper stood on edge is just the right height. Note, however, that no weight should be taken by the oil filter. Insert blocks under the exhaust manifold instead.

Next remove the rear bumper, followed by the rear cross-member of the body. This is freed by releasing the engine mounting and undoing one nut and two bolts on each side.

The fan cowl air-ducting hose and the water hoses should now be detached, followed by the complete water pump, bracket, and fan assembly. Also disconnect the electrical leads on the starter motor, the H.T. coil, the distributor L.T. terminal, and the oil and water sender units.

Now remove the starter motor securing-bolts and withdraw the unit from its housing. Disconnect the petrol pipes from the fuel pump and carburettor. Detach the air filter. Then remove the bell-housing nuts behind the engine. Finally remove the bottom nut which was previously untouched. The engine is now free from the chassis and should be carefully lifted away.

The work involved is reasonably straightforward and should pose no undue difficulties, but for detailed instructions on individual aspects of the the job, e.g. removal of the water pump, air cleaner, etc., refer to the instructions given in the appropriate chapters.

Stripping the Engine. Having thoroughly cleaned the engine externally, stripping down can begin. Follow the instructions given on pages 35 and 43 for the removal of the cylinder head and oil sump. Then detach the camshaft-drive cover. To do this, remove the crankshaft pulley and the fixing nuts around the edge of the case. Set No. 1 piston at T.D.C. firing position and draw off the case, complete with the distributor.

Interposed between the case and the cylinder block, on the right-hand side, is a rubber ring. This seals the main oil gallery at this joint and it is essential to renew it on assembly.

You should now remove the camshaft-drive chain and its tensioner, the latter being freed by pushing down on the spring to disengage its eye from the bottom moulding.

Next free the connecting-rod big-end bearing caps. Provided the engine has a satisfactory performance and oil consumption is normal, there is no need to remove the pistons and it is recommended by Chrysler that they should *not* be disturbed. Merely press them so that their crowns all come to the tops of the cylinder bores. Otherwise withdraw them and dismantle the small-ends as previously described.

Clutch Removal. First mark both the clutch assembly and the flywheel so that their balance will not be disturbed on reassembly. You should then begin undoing the six bolts which hold the clutch pressure-plate to the flywheel. Loosen each nut a little at a time, so that the spring pressure is evenly maintained on the unit. The assembly can then be detached from the car and the driven plate pulled off its splines.

With most Imp clutches this is as much as you can do because the assembly is riveted together and can only be replaced as a complete unit. This is a typical example of the modern and rather deplorable tendency of the car industry (here and abroad) to make the car owner buy parts some of which are not actually needed!

Early Imps had "built-in" diaphragm-type clutches (*see* Fig. 35) which could be stripped by detaching the cover pressing and freeing the retaining ring set in the pressure-plate abutments. This freed the diaphragm spring, the driving plate, and the pressure plate. The assembly now has to be serviced as a unit.

Oil Pump Removal. Remove the three nuts and the single cheese-headed screw which secure the base of the pump and lift it off. Place a

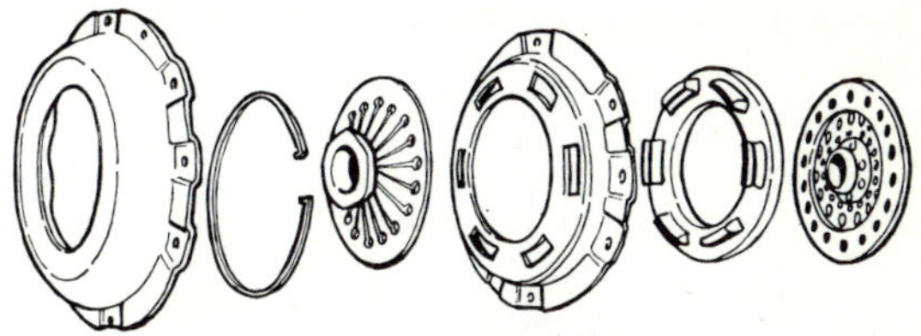

FIG. 35. THE EARLY DIAPHRAGM CLUTCH

How the various parts of the clutch are positioned is made clear on this exploded view. The later clutch units have a riveted pressure-plate assembly which you cannot dismantle.

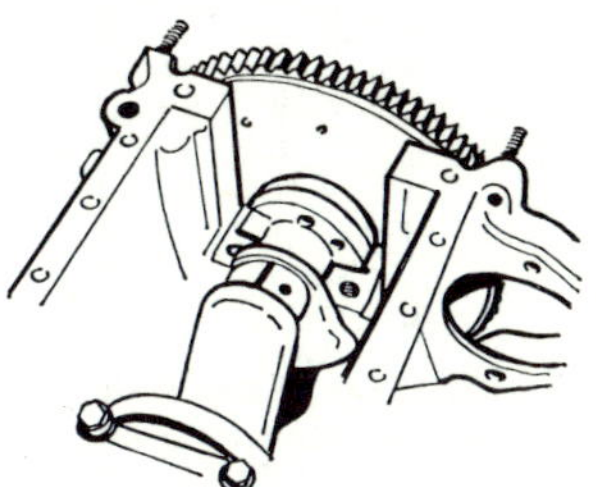

FIG. 36. THE CRANKSHAFT REAR MAIN BEARING

Unless the bearing shells are of the undowelled type (used on a few Imps) the crankshaft main bearings (three) can be renewed without removing the crankshaft, merely by pressing the worn shells out of position and the new ones in. If the rear main bearing is undowelled, the crankshaft must come out.

large washer on the screw and refit it so that the washer overlaps the pump outer rotor. This will prevent it falling off. Then pull the pump off its studs.

Removing the Crankshaft. Free the tab-washers and remove the bolts which secure the main-bearing caps, having first made sure that each cap and bolt is clearly marked for position. The crankshaft can then be lifted out (*see* Fig. 36) and the bearings withdrawn.

Recessed into the flywheel and locked by tab-washers are the bolts which secure the flywheel to the crankshaft. Flatten the tab-washers, remove the bolts, and then lift the flywheel off the crankshaft.

Distributor Removal. Pull the distributor out of its housing after removing the nuts which secure it.

Checking the Crankshaft. Have the journals and end thrust-faces inspected by a qualified agent. If the crankshaft has oval or scored journals, or its end thrust-faces are seriously worn, the crankshaft requires to be renewed.

Refitting the Crankshaft. Thoroughly clean the crankcase, paying special attention to the oilways, and allow the unit to drain dry before reassembly is commenced. This starts with the rear main-bearing cap (*see* Fig. 37)

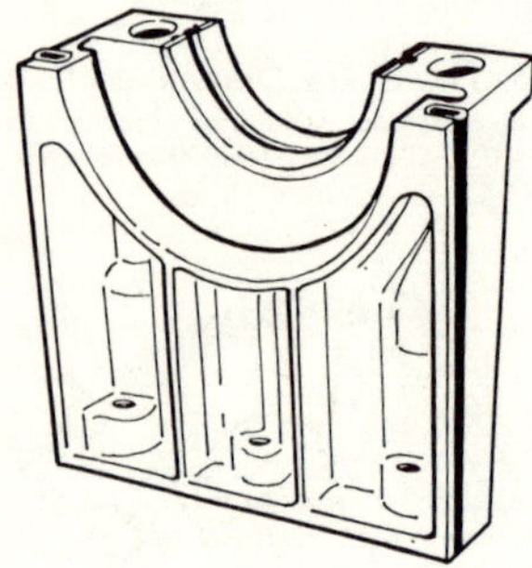

FIG. 37. THE REAR MAIN BEARING CAP

When assembling this cap, new seals must be fitted to its side grooves. Also non-setting jointing compound must be applied as explained in the text. Do not apply excessive compound, or it may block up a vital oil passage.

which has hard rubber joints with club feet to act as oil seals. Inspect the edges of the crankcase face, where the cap fits, for any sharpness which might cut the oil seals as the crankshaft is replaced. If you find any sharp edges, ease them carefully. Damage to the oil seals causes oil leakage.

Lightly smear the two corners of the rear main-bearing cap recess with non-setting jointing compound (Chrysler recommend Hylomar) but be very careful not to let any get on to the crankshaft oil-return bore or the return thread. Also smear the top of the main-bearing cap just behind the top of the side joints.

Place the crankshaft upper bearing shells (new) in their housings, lightly oil the crankshaft journals, and place the crankshaft in position. Fit the bearing caps, and re-assemble with new locking plates. Torque the cap-securing bolts to 41 lb ft.

Engine Reassembly. The remainder of the work is basically nothing more complicated than a reversal of the dismantling procedure. It should be stressed, however, that *new* gaskets, locking washers, etc., must be used throughout, and that the torque settings given for the various nuts and bolts should be studiously adhered to (*see* Appendix).

Oil Pump Replacement. As the distributor is driven through the slot in the oil-pump gear extension, correct timing demands that the oil pump should mesh in one particular position relative to its drive gear.

Fit the distributor first. Turn the crankshaft to bring No. 1 piston to T.D.C. on the firing stroke and set the distributor rotor also to the No. 1 firing position. Then re-insert the oil pump so that the small segment on its extension, viewed from the sump, is pointing to the first sump stud on the distributor side.

Alternatively, fit the oil pump first and set it so that when viewed from the distributor end the larger segment in the gear extension is pointing towards the oil-pressure sender unit.

Replacing the Clutch. Where a completely new pressure plate and friction plate assembly is being fitted this is a straightforward job, although lining-up the boss of the friction plate so that the gearbox shaft will engage calls for the use of a mandrel. This can be an old Imp shaft bought from a scrap yard; a dummy shaft made of wood; or even, at a pinch, the handle of your suction-type valve grinding tool. It should be inserted into the flywheel and the driven plate slipped along it. The mandrel should be left in place while the pressure plate is located on its dowels and bolted down. Tighten the bolts evenly, and torque them to 7 lb ft.

Rebuilding Early-type Clutch. With the old-type clutch which could be dismantled, re-assembly procedure after stripping is as follows. First smear a *little* grease (Shell Retinax A recommended by the factory) on the sides of the pressure-plate lugs, on the diaphragm spring fulcrum-points, on the driving plate, the cover, the pressure plate, and on the finger-tips where they enter the release tube. Do not over grease. Excessive grease will melt, run, get on the new friction linings of the clutch and cause slip. Just a *trace* of grease is quite sufficient.

Now place on the bench a packing piece $5\frac{1}{2}$ in. in diameter and $\frac{1}{2}$ in. deep. Insert the driving plate into its slots in the pressure plate and add the diaphragm spring, securing it with the circlip. At the factory the spring is depressed a few times in a press and the release thrust-pad is then checked for run-out with a clock gauge. The maximum amount permissible is 0·025 in. (0·65 mm).

Before adding the cover, check that the ends of the circlip fall midway between the pressure-plate lugs, and that their upturned tips face *outwards*. Then line up the cover with the locating dimples on the pressure-plate flange and reassemble the clutch to the flywheel.

The Clutch Release Bearing. This is carried on the transaxle, inside the bell housing, on a clip which is held by a single nut. Engine removal is necessary to get at the bearing. After the lever has been disconnected

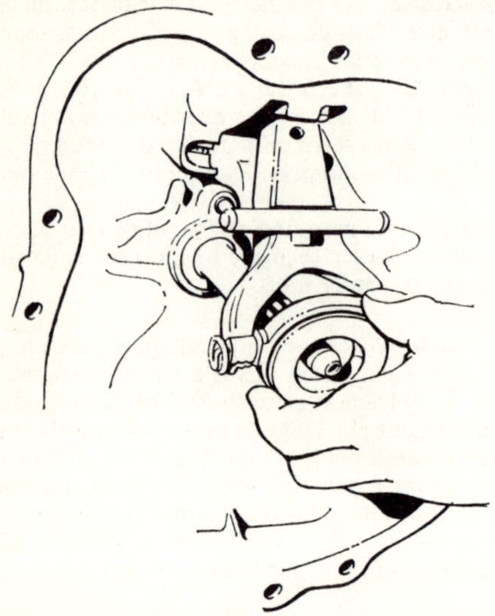

FIG. 38. THE CLUTCH RELEASE BEARING

Earlier Imp clutch release thrust bearings tended to be noisy. The later type were of modified design. The bearing can be reached only after removing the engine. Releasing one nut and the clutch rod will permit the lever and bearing to be withdrawn as shown.

from the slave cylinder's operating rod, remove the nut and pull the lever and bearing (*see* Fig. 38) away.

A common fault with the Imp is for the release bearing to become noisy once the engine heats up. This is caused by the carbon pad turning in its housing, due either to a poor fit or to loosening because of expansion. Later-type bearings have dowels inserted to locate the pad, and removing the old pad and fitting a new one should therefore effect a complete cure.

The pad itself is held to the lever by spring clips, so removal and replacement is a straightforward job. Then replace the release mechanism, linking it to the rod and finally tightening the clip bolt to 11 lb ft. To ensure smooth action it is recommended that a little Shell Retinax A be applied to the trunnions and the spring clip before assembly. There is no external means of adjustment on the operating mechanism.

Installing the Engine. Apart from the need for care in regard to one or two points, refitting the engine is done virtually in the reverse order of its removal. If the fan and water pump assembly is on the engine when it is offered up to the chassis, you must take care to avoid damaging the large rubber hose fitted between the fan and radiator cowls. When refilling the

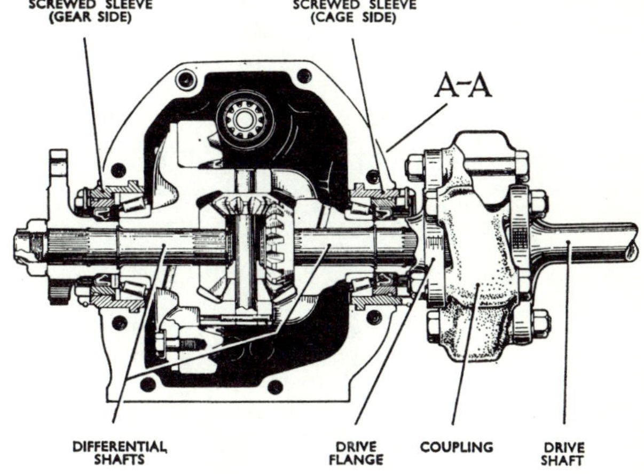

Fig. 39. Cross-sectional View of Transaxle

This shows the relationship of the driving flanges to the drive shafts. The connection is made through rubber couplings which permit the shafts to move with the rear suspension.

cooling system be sure to set the heater control to its *Red* ("On") position. After running the engine, recheck the coolant level because some of the water will have passed into the heater system. You will also have to undertake the normal heater "bleeding" procedure.

Fitting New Drive Couplings. Six bolts hold the rubber couplings (*see* Fig. 39) to the drive shaft. Remove these and detach the old couplings. Keep the rubber couplings compressed during removal (*see* Fig. 40). New couplings are supplied with a retaining clip around them to keep the rubbers compressed. Do not remove a retaining clip until the coupling to which it is fitted has been installed.

Place three bolts in the coupling in alternate holes. The head of each bolt should be *towards* the short boss of the coupling. Offer up the component to the transmission flange so that the bolts you have positioned have their heads pointing towards the transaxle (*see* Fig. 41). With the

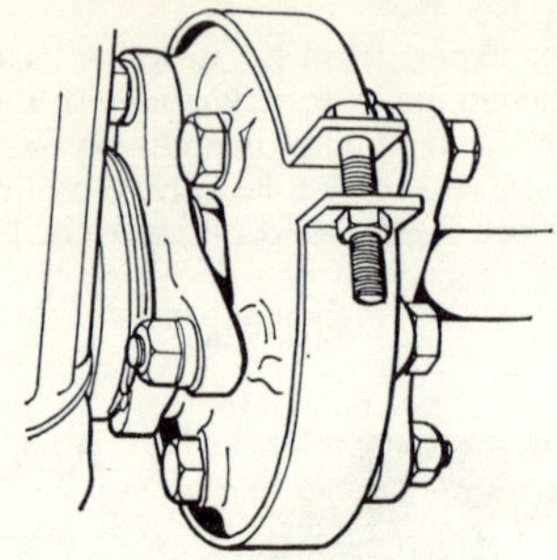

FIG. 40. A HOME-MADE DRIVE-COUPLING BAND

When removing the rubber drive-couplings, other than for complete renewal, it is advisable to make up bands as shown to keep them compressed. This will ensure that the holes will line up with those on the two flanges.

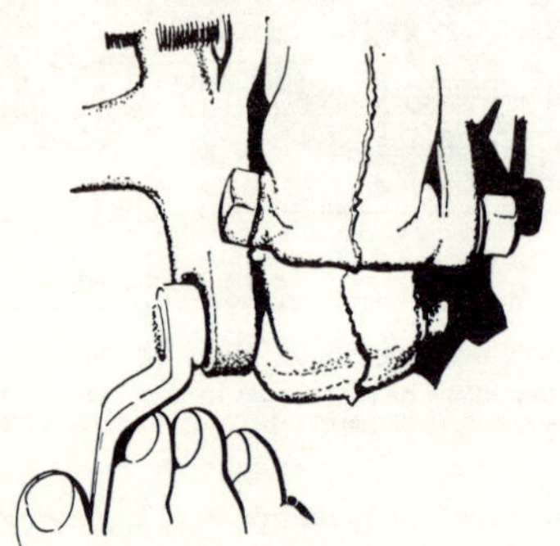

FIG. 41. REFITTING DRIVE-COUPLING BOLTS

Note than when replacing drive couplings the drive-shaft flange bolts require fitting with their heads facing the transaxle casing.

other three bolts, fix the coupling to the transmission flange. Then engage the first three bolts with the driving-shaft flange. Torque them all to 34 lb ft, and finally remove the bands from the couplings.

Crankshaft Main-bearing Shell Replacement. Except on early Imp engines (with the rear main-bearing shell not dowelled and therefore unable to be repositioned without an engine strip), the main bearing shells can be renewed with the engine installed. The procedure is as below.

Drain the oil and remove the oil sump. Remove each main-bearing cap in turn and push the *old* upper shell around the crankshaft journal for removal. Obviously it must be pushed from the side opposite to its locating lip. Then insert the shell from the lip side and press it round the journal until it seats. A new shell should be inserted into the cap, which must be fitted with a new locking plate, and the bolts tightened to 41 lb ft. The locking-plate tab should then be turned over and the other upper main-bearing shells dealt with in a similar manner.

Timing the Distributor. Turn the engine until the groove cut on the flange of the engine pulley coincides with the pointer fixed to the water pump support bracket. Then revolve the crankshaft in the normal direction of rotation until the groove is 3 mm in front of the pointer.

Set the vernier control on the distributor to its mid-way position. It is correct when two divisions are showing on the scale. Remove the distributor cap, connect a 12-volt bulb between the L.T. terminal on the distributor body and any convenient earthing point, and switch on the ignition.

Slacken the distributor clamp screw. If the bulb lights it shows that the points are open, and the distributor body should be turned anti-clockwise until it goes out again. Apply light finger pressure to the rotor in a clockwise direction, and turn the distributor body clockwise again until the bulb just lights. Then retighten the clamp.

To check the setting, turn the crankshaft two revolutions clockwise until the bulb again lights. Then note the relative positions of the pulley groove and the pointer. The distance separating them must be 3 mm. If it is, the ignition is correctly set.

Fan Belt. Twin-carburettor engines use a belt of higher quality. Any replacement belt used should be of this type, distinguished by a green mark on the outer face.

6 Work on the Electrics

PERHAPS at first sight one may be forgiven for wondering what on earth there can be in an electrical system to maintain. But second thoughts will show that there is a very considerable amount of mechanism involved. Not all the electrics, by any means, consist of static wiring.

Four essential parts of the car's electrical equipment are, in fact, basically mechanical: the distributor, the contact-breaker, the dynamo, and the starter motor. So also is the windscreen wiper mechanism. All these components require periodic attention and after varying mileages need a thorough overhaul.

Besides these there is the battery, the only chemical part of the layout. Now an Imp-sized battery cannot be overhauled—though the big batteries used on buses, for instance, are in fact rebuilt several times during their working lives. But all batteries, irrespective of size, need regular inspection and maintenance. If neglected a battery is likely to fail no less certainly than the engine if, for example, its lubrication is forgotten.

Even the wiring, static though it may be, cannot be wholly neglected. Deterioration can set in, either through age or because the harness rubs against a sharp metal edge. To guard against a possible "burn out" it is advisable to make a close visual inspection of it from time to time.

THE DISTRIBUTOR

General Maintenance. It is necessary to check the gap between the contacts of the contact-breaker at regular intervals as described on page 8 in Chapter 1. The lubrication of the contact-breaker and distributor is also dealt with there. When attending to lubrication of the contact-breaker and distributor unit be extremely careful not to allow any grease or oil to get on the contacts, and avoid excessive lubrication, or some lubricant may be thrown on to the contact-breaker contacts as the distributor operates.

Cleaning is advised at 5,000 mile intervals. Use a soft dry cloth to wipe the inside and outside of the distributor cap, paying particular attention to the space between the internal terminals. Test the H.T. pick-up in the centre of the cap. This is spring-loaded in its holder, and when it is pressed it should move freely. If it sticks, or feels stiff, remove it and find out why. There may be some dirt between the brush and the walls of the holder, or the spring may be damaged and not functioning properly.

Now take off the rotor arm (*see* Fig. 42) and examine the contact-breaker contacts. If they are badly burned and pitted it is best to fit a replacement set. Moderate surface deterioration can be rectified either

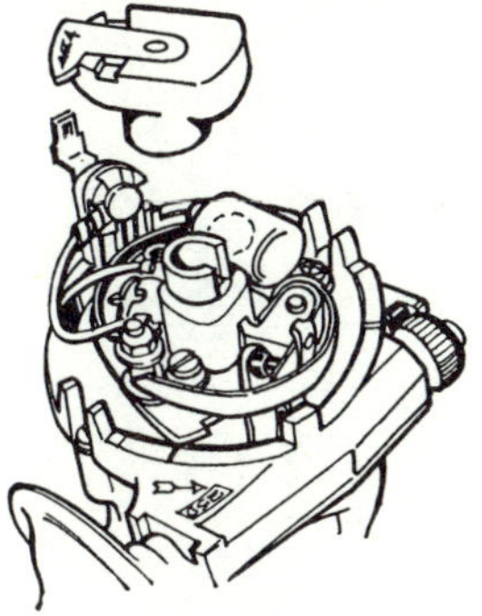

FIG. 42. THE ROTOR ARM REMOVED TO GIVE ACCESS TO THE CONTACT-BREAKER

After removing the distributor cap the rotor arm can be pulled up and out of its housing on the distributor shaft. This leaves the contact-breaker contacts accessible for inspection and adjustment.

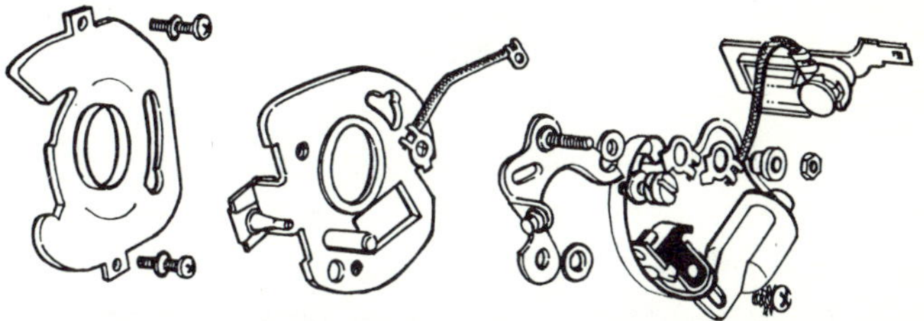

FIG. 43. EXPLODED VIEW OF LUCAS CONTACT-BREAKER

with a carborundum slip at home or, better still, on a garage's contact-refacing machine. In either case, wipe the contact-breaker absolutely clean of all metallic dust and grease afterwards by using a non-fluffy rag moistened with clean petrol.

Before replacing the contacts wipe the pivot post for the moving contact clean with a petrol-moistened rag. Then smear it lightly with some engine oil. Refit the contacts, regap them as described on page 8, and replace the rotor arm and finally the distributor cap.

Distributor Overhaul. After a very considerable mileage has been covered (about 40,000 miles) the distributor will need an overhaul. This is

FIG. 44. LUCAS CONTACT-BREAKER AND DISTRIBUTOR UNIT

This partially dismantled and exploded view shows (top to bottom): the rotor arm; the contact-breaker; the contact-breaker mounting plate; the cam unit with centrifugal advance-retard mechanism; the body, with vacuum advance-retard unit and vernier adjuster; and the distributor shaft driving dog with peg.

basically a simple procedure, and one which is quite within the ability of the average owner.

Remove the distributor unit from the engine and detach the distributor cap and rotor arm. Next free the drive-shaft dog. This is locked in position by a small locking pin inserted through the driving dog. Use a punch to tap this out, holding the body of the distributor in such a position that the smaller section of the offset is on the *left-hand side* of the distributor body, with the shaft in such a position that the rotor arm would be pointing *upwards*.

Referring to Fig. 44, free the two screws holding the contact-breaker base plate, and detach the spring from the vacuum advance-retard mechanism from its pillar on the plate. The complete base-plate assembly, including the contacts, can now be drawn out of the distributor body. Next dismantle the vacuum unit. Do this by removing with a pair of pliers the small circlip fitted on the shaft just in front of the vernier-adjuster knob; it is likely that the circlip, which is brittle, will break. Consequently it is advisable to have a spare circlip available.

Unscrew the vernier knob and pull the vacuum diaphragm unit away from the distributor body. Afterwards withdraw the shaft and bob-weights. Stripping the centrifugal mechanism is quite straightforward. Ease the advance weight-springs off their pillars on the cam plate. But be very careful not to distort them, otherwise new springs will be required for reassembly.

Fitting a New Distributor Bush. Except on an old unit, it will not usually be necessary to renew the distributor bush. Should a new bush be required, drive out the old one, taking special care not to fracture the body material. The replacement bush should have been soaked in oil for twenty-four hours before fitting. This gives it virtually life-long lubrication, although obviously it still requires small quantities of oil to be injected from time to time.

Use a stepped drift to drive in a new bush. Then, using the existing oil-hole in the body as a guide, drill its lubrication hole. Offer up the shaft. If it is an easy fit and turns without binding, all is well. If not, have the bush reamed at a garage to give the distributor shaft the required clearance.

Inspecting the Distributor Shaft. In the top of the shaft is a central set-screw which secures the cam. Release this, lift the cam, and remove the centrifugal weights. Then check the bare shaft for wear, using preferably a micrometer. It is possible, however, to employ a vernier gauge quite successfully. If obvious ovality exists it is best to fit a *new* shaft. In other cases inspect the area around the hole for the drive-dog pin. Burring frequently occurs here. If this has happened, file away any metal which is standing proud.

Reassembling the Distributor. Clean the centrifugal weights and their associated springs and plates with petrol. Allow them to drain and dry thoroughly, and then lubricate them with a molybdenum grease. Afterwards reassemble the advance-retard mechanism to the shaft and refit the cam.

Place the shaft and cam assembly back into the distributor body and rebuild the vacuum advance-retard mechanism. First offer up the diaphragm unit. Then from the other side slide on the ratchet plate and coil spring. Add the vernier knob, screwing it on until it is in the halfway position. Fit a new circlip.

Unless the existing contact-breaker contacts are in really good condition it is advisable to fit a brand-new set. Fit them to the base plate. Be sure that you do not get the fibre washers mixed up when doing this. Then replace the distributor leads.

Now lightly coat the cam with the recommended grease (Shell Retinax A) and offer up the complete base-plate to the distributor body. Where a vacuum unit is fitted, remember to hook its spring on to the pillar as you do this. Reconnect the earth lead, and gap the contact-breaker contacts. This is very easily done at this stage. Just turn the distributor shaft until the heel of the fibre contact-breaker arm is riding on the peak of the cam; then adjust the gap to 0·015 in. and replace the rotor arm.

Finally fit the driving dog. Turn the rotor arm so that it lines up with the L.T. terminal, the contact plate on the arm pointing towards it. Position the dog so that the smaller offset is on the *left* side and drive home the locking pin. Replace and time the distributor unit.

THE DYNAMO

Lubrication. About every 12,000 miles or once a year (whichever is the most frequent) inject a few drops of clean *engine oil* through the hole marked "Oil" which you will find at the commutator end of the Lucas dynamo. Apart from this (*see* Fig. 45) the dynamo requires no lubrication at all between overhauls.

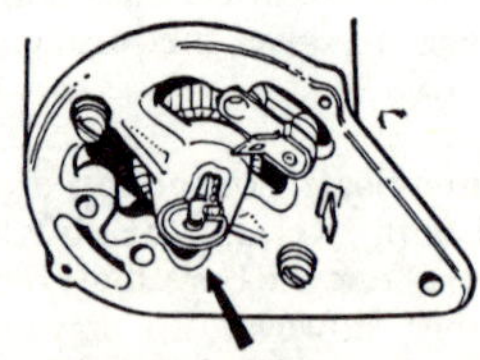

FIG. 45. LUBRICATION POINT FOR DYNAMO REAR BEARING

The front bearing of the dynamo is pre-packed with grease and needs no attention. The rear bearing must be oiled at 12,000 mile intervals. Lubricant must be injected through the hole in the boss shown above.

The Commutator Brushes. Remove the dynamo from the engine. To do this, disconnect the *D* and *F* terminals and detach the fan belt. Unscrew the three bolts which secure the dynamo to its bracket on the cylinder head.

With the dynamo on the bench detach the driving pulley and remove the

terminals from "output" and "field" connections. Then unscrew the two
through-bolts (*see* Fig. 46) which hold the dynamo end-plates. As these
bolts are withdrawn, remove the brush housing. Then detach the driving-
end bracket and the armature assembly from the yoke.

Test the brushes by lifting each into its brush box and hold it there by
slipping the spring on to the side of its brush. Fit the commutator end-
bracket over the commutator, and release the brushes.

Hold back each brush spring in turn and gently move the brush thus
freed, tugging gently on its flexible connector. It should move freely. If it

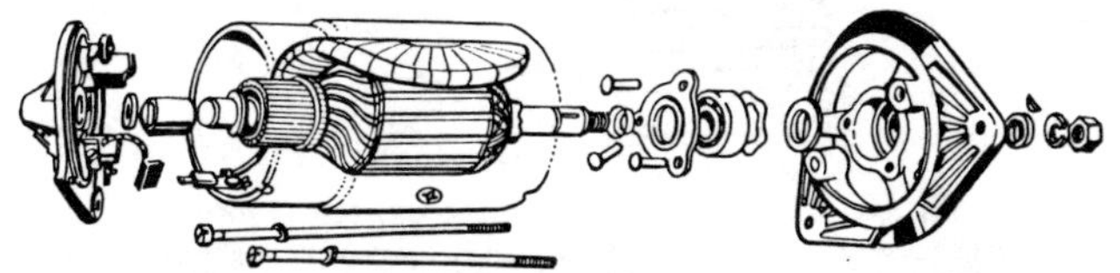

FIG. 46. EXPLODED VIEW OF PARTLY DISMANTLED LUCAS DYNAMO
Detaching the through-bolts allows the end plates to be taken off the yoke, and the
armature to be withdrawn from the dynamo for attention.

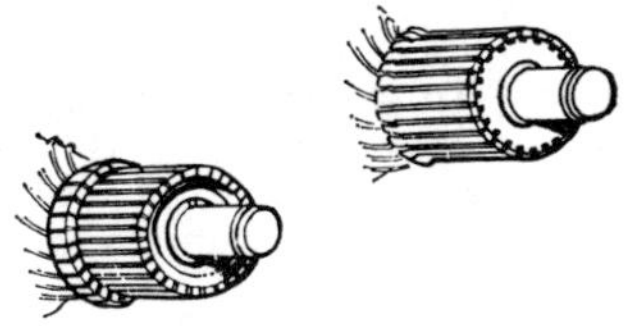

FIG. 47. DYNAMO COMMUTATORS FITTED TO IMPS
Two different types have been used. That shown on the left is the older version; on the
right is the later moulded component.

does not, remove the brush completely from its holder and lightly ease its
sides with a smooth file.

Where brushes are obviously badly worn they must be renewed and the
replacements properly bedded down. To do this, wrap *medium-grade*
glasspaper (with the abrasive side upwards) around the commutator;
press the working surface of the brush on to it while rotating the commutator. This grinds away the carbon of the brush until its contour
exactly matches that of the commutator segments. On the Hillman Imp
the minimum permissible length of each brush is $\frac{9}{32}$ in. (7 mm).

Recutting Armature. In time the process of wear and tear on the armature results in its metal segments no longer standing sufficiently proud

from the insulation. When this stage is reached the insulated sections must be cut back (*see* Fig. 48). A section of hacksaw blade broken off

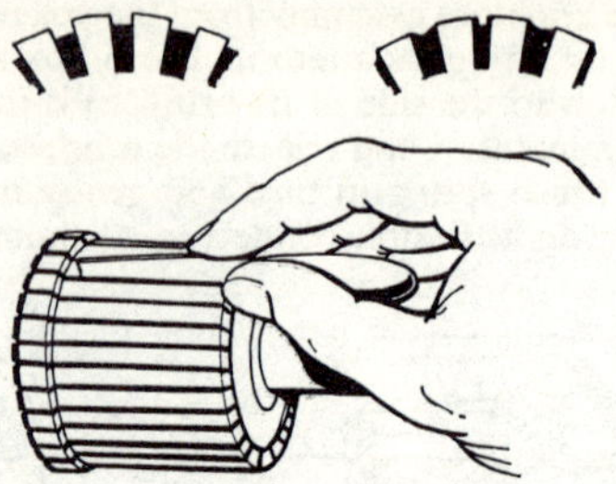

FIG. 48. CUTTING-BACK THE COMMUTATOR GROOVES

If the grooves between the segments have worn like those in the right-hand inset, they must be relieved until they appear like those on the left. You can make up a cutting tool from a piece of hacksaw blade.

squarely will be found a suitable tool for this work. It is essential that the job is done cleanly and that the cuts follow the actual wedge shape of the segments.

Refitting the Brushgear. To remove the brushgear the end plate must be taken off the dynamo. As the Imp dynamo is "windowless," a particular method of refitting the brushgear must be used. Before replacing the end plate, lift each brush and trap it with the spring, as during normal

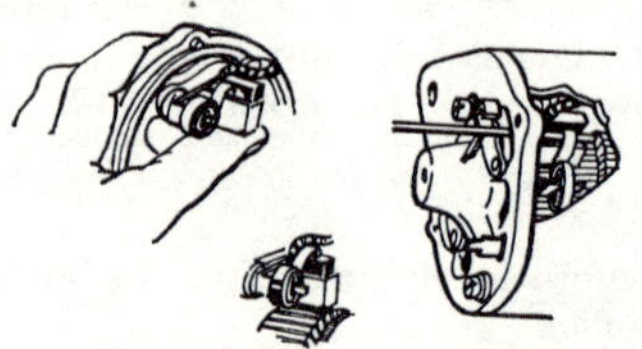

FIG. 49. REFITTING COMMUTATOR BRUSHES

Using a piece of rod to replace the brushes as explained in the text.

inspection. Offer up the plate with the brushes raised and refit the two through-bolts. Then insert through the end slots a length of steel rod of a diameter small enough to enter the rolled end of the spring, and in turn release the pressure of the spring on each brush (*see* Fig. 49). The brush will slide down its holder, and the spring can then be released to take up its normal position on the top of the brush.

THE STARTER MOTOR

Testing the Starter Motor in Position. Where starter trouble is encountered there are several possibilities which can be checked very easily with the starter motor still in position, assuming that the battery is fully charged.

Switch on the lamps and operate the starter, listening carefully. If the lamps dim but you cannot hear the starter operating, this indicates that the current is flowing through the armature's windings but that the armature of the starter motor is not rotating. If the engine is not abnormally stiff (as it would be, for instance, following a piston seizure), the probability is that the starter pinion has become permanently meshed with the ring gear. This could happen as the result of the starter being operated with the engine running.

If, on the other hand, the lamps retain full brilliance when the starter is operated, either the supply circuit is broken or else there is an internal fault in the starter motor itself.

Where the starter action is very sluggish there is a possibility that the fault lies in a loose connection, with consequent high resistance in the circuit. A fast starter action which does not rotate the engine indicates positively that the drive is damaged.

Removing the Starter Motor. Even if starting trouble is non-existent, about every 15,000 miles the starter motor should be removed from the engine for stripping and inspection. Before attempting to do this *disconnect the leads from the battery terminals*. Failure to do this may result in a short-circuit and can lead to a very nasty burn and damage.

Next disconnect the main lead from the starter motor and take out the two bolts which hold it to the clutch housing. Pull the starter motor clear. Should it stick, it can be jarred loose by gentle tapping with a wooden block.

Stripping the Starter Motor. First remove the clamp-type metal strap from the commutator end of the body ("yoke") and lift the brush-retaining springs. Holding each back (*see* Fig. 50), lift the brushes from their holders.

Take the nuts off the terminal post which protrudes from the commutator-end bracket and unscrew the two through-bolts (*see* Fig. 51). The bracket should now be detached from the yoke. The driving-end bracket will then come away, together with the armature. You may find a thrust washer on the commutator end of the shaft. If so, be careful not to lose it.

Cleaning the Commutator. If it is to operate efficiently, the commutator must be clean, and not fouled by oil, grease, or dirt. Loose dirt can be removed with a soft clean cloth, more stubborn dirt with a cloth dipped in petrol. Where contamination is particularly bad, wrap a piece of fine glasspaper (not emery cloth) around the commutator, and around this wind a strap formed from a length of stout rag. With the commutator held firmly in a padded vice, pull the ends of the strap up and down. This will rotate the glasspaper and thus polish the commutator segments. Unlike the dynamo, the insulation between the segments of a starter motor must *never* be undercut.

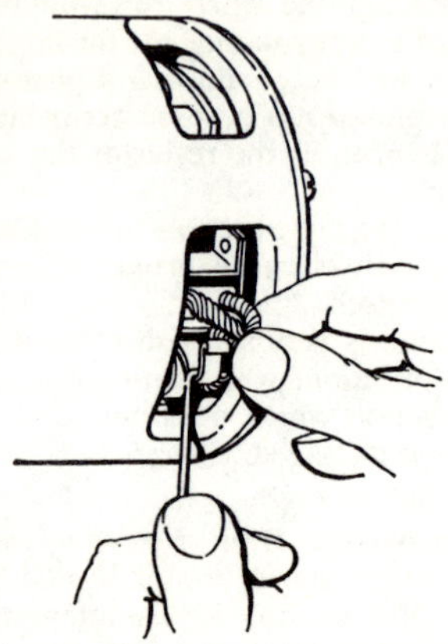

FIG. 50. WITHDRAWING COMMUTATOR BRUSH

Unlike the dynamo, where stripping down is necessary before the brushes can be inspected, the starter motor has "windows" covered by a clamp-type metal strap. By hooking back the retaining spring each brush can be freed and gently eased out of its box for inspection.

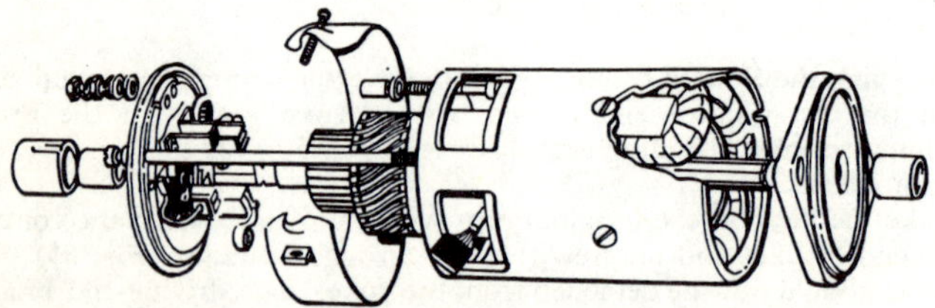

FIG. 51. EXPLODED AND PARTLY CUT-AWAY VIEW OF THE STARTER MOTOR

This drawing shows how the starter motor can be dismantled for overhaul after releasing the through-bolts which secure its ends.

Commutator Brush Removal. Brush wear is very limited, but if starting trouble develops remove (*see* Fig. 50) and inspect each brush for wear. If wear of a brush has reached the stage where it no longer bears on the commutator segments, or if wear is so pronounced that sections of the flexible connection are exposed on its contact face, renewal is necessary. Brushes should, of course, always be inspected when the starter motor is stripped.

It may be best, if a flexible connection is exposed, to entrust repair work to a qualified auto-electrician. In an emergency, however, it *can* be done at home if great care is taken with the soldering. The following is the method to adopt.

Cut cleanly through the flexible connection $\frac{1}{8}$ in. (3 mm) away from the aluminium. Clean up and tin the original resistance-brazed joint. Then take the replacement brush unit, and open up the loop in its flexible connection. Tin this, but be absolutely sure that you do not allow any solder to run towards the brush.

Offer up the brush unit to the original connection, placing the joint within the loop. Then squeeze up the loop and make a strong soldered joint. Repeat the sequence for any other brushes which require to be replaced in this manner. There is, by the way, no need to bed new brushes on the commutator segments because they are pre-formed during manufacture.

Rebuilding the Starter Motor. Replace the armature and end-cap assembly (*see* Fig. 51) into the yoke, check that the thrust washer has been refitted and then add the commutator-end bracket, threading the commutator brushes through the "windows" in the yoke. Some mechanics prefer to fit the commutator-end bracket first, believing that this makes it easier to position the brushes.

Replace the fibre and steel washers on the terminal post, fit the nut, and replace and tighten the two through-bolts. Then slip the brushes back into their holders and secure them with their springs. Replace the cover plate.

The Starter Drive. This is another of those infuriating "sealed" assemblies which can only be serviced as a unit. In the event of a fault, the complete barrel must be renewed. If this is done, it is recommended that the screwed sleeve should also be replaced by a new part. Periodically clean the drive dog by washing it in petrol and, after draining, brushing it lightly with paraffin.

THE BATTERY

Although a battery needs little maintenance, the modest servicing it requires must be done regularly if its life is not to be drastically reduced. During use evaporation takes place within its cells. What is lost is not the working electrolyte, but part of its water content. This must be made good.

Topping-up the Battery. In the summer (especially in hot weather) check the electrolyte level *weekly*. In winter checking once a fortnight suffices. The electrolyte in each cell should be *just above the tops of the plates* inside the battery case; the level can be observed when the battery filler-plugs are removed. If the level is below the recommended level, top-up with distilled water as required, using a syringe or battery filler. You can buy distilled water in bulk from a chemist, and this is much cheaper than obtaining it in dribs and drabs from a garage. *Never* use tap water which contains impurities likely to damage the battery cells. In an emergency (where you find the electrolyte level seriously low, with no distilled water available) you can add water obtained by defrosting the freezer compartment of a domestic refrigerator.

Do not be led into topping-up the cells excessively. If you do this, electrolyte will be forced out and probably damage the surrounding car metal-work.

Corrosion. The Imp battery is prone to corrosion. Periodically remove it, and neutralize deposits on the battery terminals and on the car body-work adjacent to the battery carrier. Do this with a strong solution of bicarbonate of soda, which will form a neutral salt with the partly acid deposit. Wash and dry the metal afterwards, applying priming paint, and then a top coat. When this has dried, brush on a heavy coat of rubberized sealing-compound to provide more lasting protection.

Wash the battery terminals and casing with a bicarbonate of soda solution also, and sponge away any dirt and deposits from the battery top with a cloth damped with it. Obviously no solution must be allowed to enter the battery cells. When the terminals are clean smear them liberally with silicone grease or petroleum jelly; replace the battery, reconnect its leads (whose terminals should also be smeared with silicone grease or petroleum jelly after being neutralized), and fit the battery securing strap. If after washing, the terminals are dull in appearance, their contact surfaces should be brightened with fine emery cloth before the grease or petroleum jelly is applied. The same applies to the battery posts.

State of Charge. Taking specific gravity (S.G.) readings in each battery cell with a hydrometer will tell you exactly in what state of charge the battery cell is. The hydrometer float should indicate 1·250 for a fully-charged cell, and 1·190–1·120 for a cell in a very poor state of charge. S.G. readings above 1·250 indicate overcharging, especially if such readings are combined with a need for frequent topping-up, burned-out bulbs, etc. If such annoying symptoms occur, drive the car to an auto-electrician for a full electrical check-up, rather than attempt to diagnose the trouble yourself.

THE LUCAS LAMPS

Keep Your Lamps Clean. Always keep the glass lenses of all lamps thoroughly clean. Wash chromium-plated rims and dry them with a damp chamois leather. Then apply chrome cleaner, and afterwards polish them with a soft duster. Polish exposed chrome surfaces with a good wax polish.

The Two Headlamps. Each headlamp (*see* Fig. 52) has a "sealed beam" Lucas light-unit. To remove this, release the bayonet mounting and then

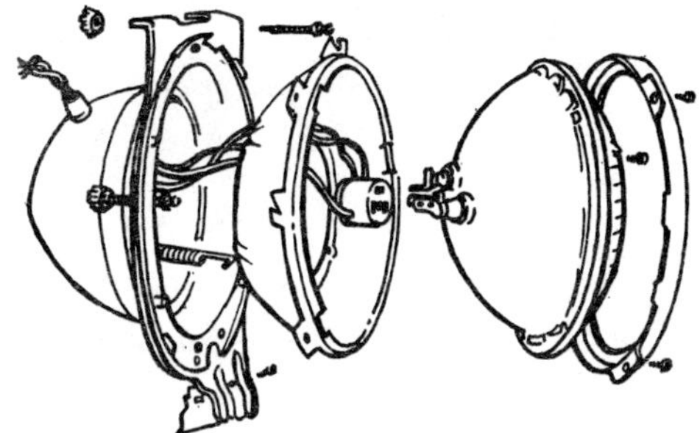

FIG. 52. A DISMANTLED HEADLAMP

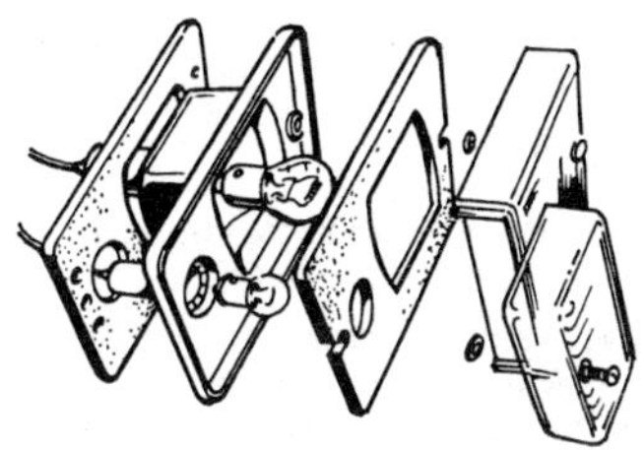

FIG. 53. A DISMANTLED SIDE- AND FLASHER-LAMP

separate the parts by loosening the securing screws. The light unit, in Britain, is a Lucas No. 5041043.

The Front Side and Flasher Lamps. Each of these two lamps (*see* Fig. 53) is provided with two sealing glands to prevent the entry of water. One gland is located behind the lamp and the other between the lamp body and lens. To obtain access to the bulbs, remove the two glass lenses. The correct bulbs to fit are a Lucas No. 989 or 222 for the side light, and a Lucas No. 382 for the flasher (front and rear).

The Rear and Indicator Lamps. Two of these lamps are, of course, fitted each side. If you wish to remove a complete lamp unit as shown in Fig. 54, free the snap connector and remove the lamp securing-screws from inside the engine compartment. If you want only to withdraw the

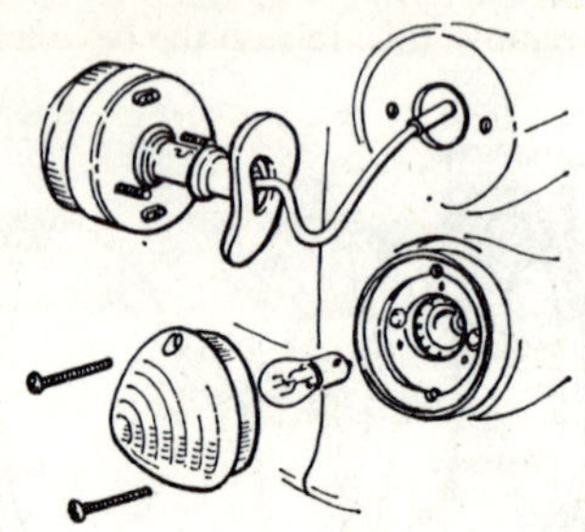

FIG. 54. A DISMANTLED STOP-TAIL LAMP

FIG. 55. THE REAR NUMBER-PLATE LAMP DISMANTLED

lens for bulb renewal, remove from the outside the two through-bolts which pass through the lens. The correct stop-tail lamp bulb to fit is a Lucas No. 380. For the indicators, use Lucas No. 382 bulbs.

The Rear Number-plate Lamp. To obtain access to the bulb of this single lamp shown in Fig. 55, remove the two screws securing the lens. If bulb renewal is necessary, fit a Lucas No. 207.

7 The cooling system

PROVIDED the necessary minimum of care is given to it, and the correct anti-freeze (Bluecol AA) is used in winter, the Imp's cooling system should be both efficient and reliable.

GENERAL MAINTENANCE

Flushing the System. An essential part of general maintenance is to flush the cooling system thoroughly at the end of the winter. To do this, set the heater control to "Red," remove the radiator filler-cap, and completely remove both drain taps. One is on the cylinder block; the other is sited at the bottom of the radiator. Allow the coolant to drain away completely.

Draining can be done with the engine either hot or cold, but if it is hot you must take great care not to scald yourself when removing the radiator filler-cap. First release it half a turn to its safety lock position. Then, keeping the orifice covered with a thick rag, remove the cap completely.

If the engine is not already cold, you should now allow it to cool before the next operation. This is to insert a hosepipe into the radiator and force water through the entire cooling system, so that it carries away any impurities out through the drain-tap holes. Continue flushing until the water issuing from the holes is absolutely clean. You can then turn off the hose, permit the remaining water to drain away, replace the drain taps, and refill the cooling system.

"Bleeding" the Heater. When the cooling system has been drained and refilled, it is likely that air will have been trapped in the long pipes which connect the heater core with the main cooling passages. "Bleeding" will therefore be needed to rectify this. If this is not done the heater will not become properly warmed up.

Release the trim pad at the rear of the boot, and you will uncover the heater valve (*see* Fig. 56) on the front bulkhead. Connect to this a length of rubber tubing and immerse its other end in a jar containing one pint of coolant. This should be the same coolant as you are using in the rest of the system. Therefore if anti-freeze has been added to the main supply, the jar should also contain its due proportion of anti-freeze. The jar should also be big enough to contain at least another half-pint of coolant over and above the pint already in it. Set the heater control to "Red," and top-up the main coolant system until the water level reaches the over-flow pipe in the header tank. Then start the engine and run it at about

2,000 r.p.m.—a little faster than a fast idle—and watch the coolant level. Starting the engine will cause this to drop, so top it up again. Then, with the engine still running, move to the front of the car and operate the vent tap. Fluid will then be pumped into the jar. Keep the tap open until the coolant emerging from the pipe is free of air bubbles. Then close the tap and suddenly open the throttle to speed up the engine. Follow this by opening the tap once more and "bleeding" again. If the coolant is still clear, shut the tap, again speed up the engine, and the process is complete.

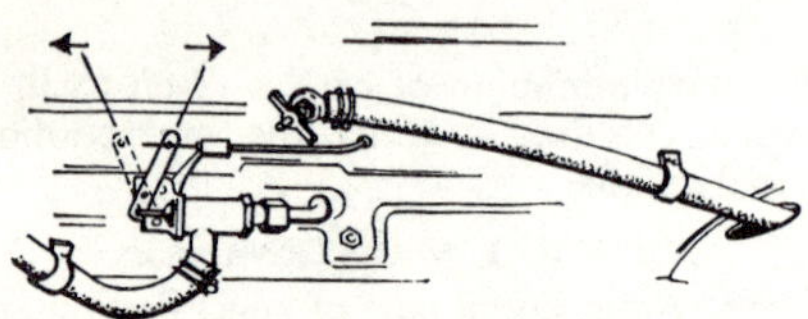

FIG. 56. THE HEATER CONTROL

When the bulkhead trim in the front luggage compartment is released the heater control is accessible. The lever operates the water valve, and the "bleed" valve is the tap located on the pipe above the control.

Replace the radiator filler-cap, stop the engine, and remove the rubber pipe. Slip back the trim pad behind its tabs, and discard the coolant in the jar.

Thermostat Removal. To keep the engine at its correct operating temperature and to ensure that it reaches it as quickly as possible, a thermostat is fitted in a housing at the forward end of the cylinder head. It is a heat-sensitive valve which opens fully when the surrounding coolant has reached operating temperature. Until then, circulation of the coolant is confined within the cylinder jackets, the cylinder head, and the water pump. When the valve opens the coolant is allowed to pass through the radiator as well.

Obtaining access to the thermostat is tricky. It involves draining the cooling system as already described, blocking up the rear of the car so that you can crawl underneath, and removing the vertical metal shield at the front of the engine compartment. This is held by five cross-headed screws. You can then reach the thermostat housing which is held on its studs by two nuts. Release these, draw off the housing, and the thermostat can be eased out of position (*see* Fig. 57).

Testing the Thermostat. For this you will need a thermometer which records in the 150°–200°F range, a pan, a stick, and a length of wire. Loop the wire round one of the body members of the thermostat and hang it from the stick so that it is suspended in the water in the pan. Heat this, measuring its temperature with the thermometer. The thermostat valve should begin to open at between 170° and 179°F. If it does not, a new one will be needed. Do not let either the thermostat or the thermometer touch the pan, or you will get a false reading.

Refitting the Thermostat. Ensure that the mating faces of the cylinder head and the thermostat housing are clean, and are not damaged. Place the thermostat in its housing, slip a new gasket over the studs, and replace

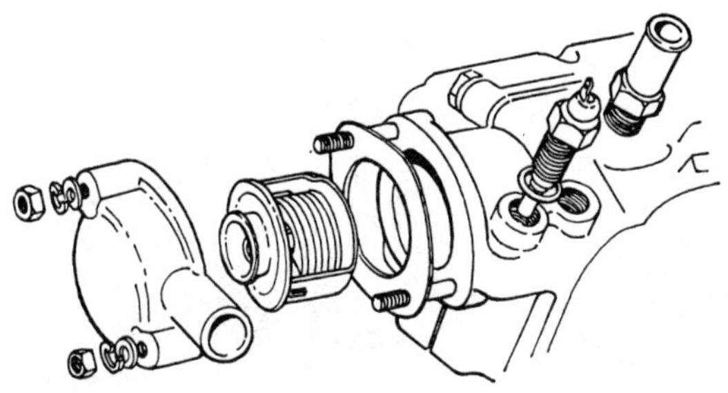

FIG. 57. THE THERMOSTAT AND ITS HOUSING

The thermostat, which should be checked at least once a year, is set in a housing at the end of the cylinder head. The housing also contains the electric sensor for the water-temperature warning light.

the cover. Torque the nuts to 6 lb ft; refit the metal shield and refill and "bleed" the cooling system.

Cleaning the Radiator. Externally the Imp radiator tends to get rather dirty in use, and it pays to keep a check on the condition of the core. If inspection suggests that the gills are becoming blocked it can be blown clear with a garage air-line.

Severe blockage calls for the removal of the radiator, however. Drain the cooling system; disconnect the feed and return hoses at the radiator end; then slacken the innermost wire clip holding the large rubber shroud to the fan cowling. Remove from the adjacent vertical panel the three cross-headed screws which retain the radiator stone guard. Then detach the three holding bolts (one each side of the header tank and one at the left-hand side of the cylinder block) and withdraw the radiator from the car. This is done from underneath. It cannot be removed from above. Fig. 58 shows details of the radiator assembly.

Stand the radiator against a wall and hose the gills clear. Better still, fill a bath with very hot water containing a mild detergent and scrub them free of dirt, using a stiff bristle brush. Never use a wire brush. This might damage the thin metal of the gills. When the radiator core is clear, use a tyre pump to blow away the remaining traces of detergent and then allow the radiator to drain completely.

Reverse Flushing. While you have the radiator off, take the chance of reverse flushing it. Connect a hose to the bottom radiator-feed pipe and force water through so that it emerges from the filler cap orifice. This will free deposits which ordinary flushing leaves untouched.

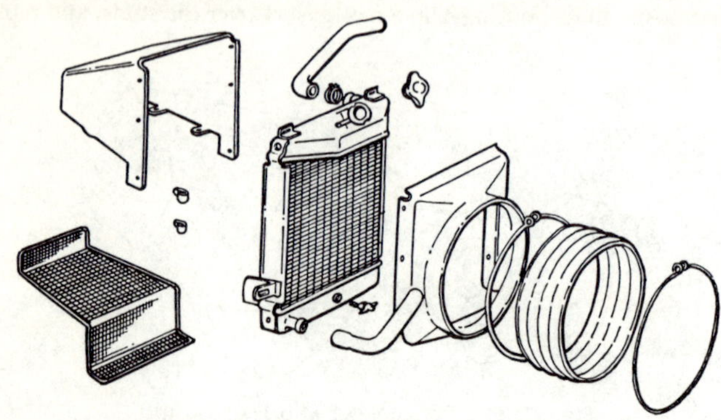

FIG. 58. THE RADIATOR ASSEMBLY DISMANTLED

Periodically the Imp radiator must be removed for thorough cleansing. The component parts and their order of assembly are indicated above.

Refit the radiator by reversing the removal procedure. You will, of course, have to carry out the normal refilling and "bleeding" also.

THE WATER PUMP

How to Remove it. Should the water pump need to come off for reconditioning, drain the cooling system and remove the fan belt. Slacken the nut on the retaining bolt of the rubber shroud on the fan cowl and slide the clip over so that it is alongside the second clip. Then remove the dynamo, having first released its spade connectors.

Free the hoses from the radiator, cylinder block, water-pump bypass, and then remove the three long bolts which hold the bracket assembly to the cylinder block. You can then lift the complete pump and fan assembly from the car and take it to the bench.

Dismantling the Water Pump. Detach the cooling fan by unscrewing its three retaining bolts from the triangular driving member. There may be distance pieces interposed. If so, note their positions for reassembly.

Remove the four long bolts which pass through the pump's inlet and outlet bodies and unscrew the large nuts placed at each end of the impeller spindle. Draw off the driving member and the driving pulley. Both of these are keyed. An exploded view of the water pump is shown in Fig. 59.

Holding one half of the pump body steady, you should now turn the other, at the same time pulling it outwards. When the two halves have been separated take out the sealing joint-washer. The pump and impeller unit (which cannot be broken down) can now be withdrawn and, if necessary, the spring-loaded water seals detached. To remove the bearings, heat the pump case gently and then drive its bearings out with a soft drift.

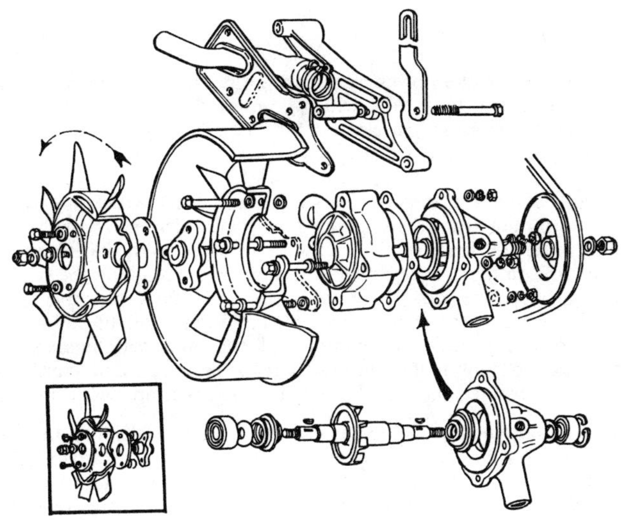

FIG. 59. EXPLODED VIEW OF WATER PUMP AND FAN ASSEMBLY

The inset shows a radiator fan of early type. The pump impeller is integral with the pump shaft, and it cannot be removed. The whole unit must be replaced where necessary.

Reassembly of the Water Pump. In general, this merely entails reversing the procedure used for stripping. Note that if the pump impeller and spindle assembly is damaged it must be replaced by a completely new unit, because the components are matched at the factory. The latest pumps also have pressure-balanced seals. These are not interchangeable with earlier types.

Before fitting the two halves of the pump body together, coat the mating faces with Shell Ensis Fluid 256. Besides being a safeguard against corrosion, this treatment will make it easier to dismantle the pump on any future occasion. Note that it is vital to refit the four spacing washers which are placed between the hub of the fan cowl and the pump's outlet body. These washers go on the four long bolts which pass through both shells. All nuts and bolts should be torqued to 6 lb ft.

8 The fuel system and carburettors

THE fuel system of the Imp is quite conventional. At the front of the car is an oblong petrol tank, into which is inserted a fuel pipe and a filter. Also in the tank is the sender element for the fuel gauge, a form of rheostat operated by the arm and a float.

The Imp Layout in a Nutshell. Fuel is induced into the fuel pipe by means of a pump mounted on the engine. This pump, driven by a cam on the camshaft, pressure-feeds fuel from the petrol tank to the carburettor, the pump incorporating a device which prevents it overcoming the resistance of the carburettor's float assembly when the float chamber is full. Generally speaking, the result is a simple and utterly reliable layout which normally calls for the very minimum of care and maintenance. This, however, does not imply that the system requires *no* care and maintenance. It does for several reasons, and keeping the system clean is *very* important.

Why Cleaning the Fuel System is Essential. Petrol delivered direct from a garage pump is not a clinically pure liquid, no matter how carefully it is handled. All petrol pumps are fed from huge underground tanks, and there is invariably a small water content in the fuel. Most of this sinks to the bottom of the car's fuel tank (the reason why the tank pick-up is so located that it does not draw out the last dregs of petrol), but some inevitably gets conveyed into the rest of the fuel system.

All fuel also contains small solid impurities, the main reason why filters are incorporated. Again, although the filters trap most impurities, a proportion does in fact reach the carburettor, and after a considerable mileage, about 15,000 miles, some at least of its jets become scored by the passage of minute pieces of grit. Thereafter the carburettor no longer gives of its best; and further down the system the fuel pump and tank filters steadily become restricted as dirt builds up in them. At the bottom of the petrol tank the trapped water eventually sets up corrosion if air can also reach the metal; it may, for example, if the fuel level is allowed to fall so low that the tank is virtually empty. Hence cleaning the fuel system periodically must be regarded as an essential item of maintenance.

Carburettor Overhaul. Cleaning and, if necessary, adjustment and overhaul of the carburettor, at intervals of about 15,000 miles is *extremely* important. If there is no undue wear in the carburettor casting, a new throttle assembly, jets, gaskets, etc., will suffice. Where the metal in the body of the instrument has, however, become ridged it is preferable to hand in the old instrument for an exchange unit. After fitting a new or reconditioned carburettor it is always advisable to check, and if necessary adjust, the contact-breaker and sparking-plug gaps, so that the improved efficiency of carburation is not offset by an out-of-tune ignition system. The cleaning, adjustment and maintenance of the Solex carburettor is dealt with on pages 78–86, and of the Stromberg on pages 86–94.

A.C. FUEL PUMP MAINTENANCE

The Pump Filter. Every 2,500 miles the filter should be examined, and cleaned if necessary. It is located below the top cover (*see* Fig. 60) which is held by a single screw. Remove this, and lift the filter from its seating and clean it thoroughly by swilling it in petrol. At the same time flush out any sediment which is trapped in the fuel-pump chamber.

Before refitting the pump cover it is vital to ensure that its rubber washer is in good condition. If this is damaged it should not be used again but replaced by a new one. Remember also to fit the fibre washer under the head of the securing screw, and to tighten the screw itself enough to make a petrol-proof joint. But do not overdo it, because the screw is threaded into *soft* metal and if you apply too much force you will undoubtedly strip the body threads.

Stripping the Fuel Pump. Disconnect the petrol pipes at their inlet and outlet unions and remove the two nuts securing the pump to the engine crankcase. The A.C. pump can then be lifted away. An exploded view illustrating all its main components is shown in Fig. 60.

Make a vertical mark across the joint between the top and bottom castings of the pump with a file. This will aid reassembly. Then wash the pump thoroughly in clean petrol before dismantling begins. Remove the screws which hold the two castings together. The lower half contains the diaphragm mechanism. The diaphragm and pull rod can then be detached by turning the mechanism through ninety degrees and lifting it away from the lower casting.

It is usual to practise preventive replacement of the pump's diaphragm assembly whenever the unit is dismantled. In any case it should be noted that where the top of the pull-rod is rivetted to the top washer no attempt should be made to separate the diaphragm layers from the protective washers and the pull rod. All gaskets should also be renewed.

Wash the area around the valves in the upper casting in a paraffin bath and examine both halves for any cracks or other damage. Inspect the filter cover, and if it proves to be distorted inwards around the centre hole, renew it. A badly corroded filter gauze should also be renewed, as should the diaphragm springs. These springs are colour-coded for strength, and it is vital that the colour of the original springs (or the number stamped on the pump flange) should be quoted when obtaining a replacement.

Examine the valves, springs, and seats for deterioration, and the link engagement slots for wear. Worn rocker-pin holes mean that the pin must

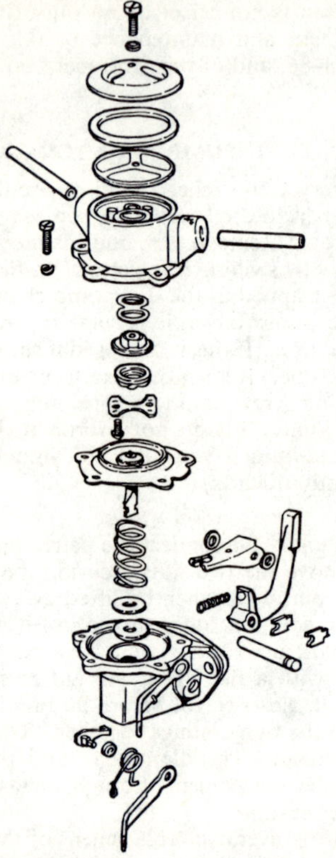

FIG. 60. EXPLODED VIEW OF A.C. FUEL PUMP

Pressure is adjusted by varying the thickness of the packing shims interposed between the pump and its cambox mounting.

be peened to give a tighter fit. Invariably the rocker-arm spring should be replaced, and wear at the point where the rocker arm makes contact with the link must not be greater than to permit a slight slackness when fitted to the rocker-arm pin.

Fuel Pump Reassembly. Where the valves, springs, and seats are held in the upper casting by a retaining plate and screws, ensure that the "8" shaped gasket is in place before the assemblies are fitted. The spring for the inlet valve must be fitted protruding into the chamber, while the outlet valve should be fitted in the reverse position so that it will allow a flow of fuel out of the pump. Afterwards, fit the retaining plate and tighten its two screws.

Assemble the link, packing washers, rocker arm, and rocker pin in the lower half of the pump body. Fitting of the rocker pin can be simplified by first inserting a piece of 0·24 in. diameter rod through the pin hole on one side of the body. Press it in far enough to engage the rocker arm washers and link. Then enter the rocker-arm pin from the other side, easing out the temporary pivot as the pin takes up position.

Where the pump has an oil seal, fit this and its spring on to the pull-rod and turn the washer through ninety degrees to hold it in place. Position the diaphragm assembly over the spring (pull-rod pointing downwards), and centre the upper end of the spring in the lower protective washer. As you press down on the diaphragm, turn the assembly to the left to set the push-rod in its correct working position relative to the link. This will take a quarter of a turn. It will enable the pull-rod slots to engage with the fork on the link, and will also align the holes in the diaphragm with those on the pump body. Note that when first placing the diaphragm assembly in the body the locating tab will be in the eleven o'clock position.

You can now assemble the pump. Push the rocker arm towards the pump until the diaphragm is level with the body flanges, and then place the upper half of the pump on top, aligning the marks made before stripping.

Fit the screws and lock washers and tighten them just sufficiently for the screw heads to engage on the washers. Now slip a 4 in. length of tube over the end of the rocker and press the arm away from the pump. This will hold the diaphragm at the top of its stroke. Keep up the pressure so that the diaphragm remains there while the cover screws are fully tightened, working from one screw to that diagonally opposite.

Pumps which are fitted with rocker-arm stop screws and washers must have these parts removed during the operation just described. When the two halves are securely mated refit the stops.

Note that when matching-up is correct the diaphragm edge should be more or less flush with the two clamping faces. If there is any appreciable protrusion the job must be done again, and special care taken to keep the downward pressure on the arm during final tightening of the screws.

Fuel Pump Troubles. There are about half a dozen possible troubles which may occur with the fuel pump. Fuel starvation at high speeds can be attributed mainly to general wear and tear in an old pump, or to air leaks caused by loose unions or damaged or over-compressed cork filter gaskets.

Fairly closely associated with fuel starvation is difficult starting caused by slow priming. It can often be due to leakage or wear, faulty valves, or a diaphragm which is insufficiently flexed. But it is also possible that the fault may lie in the carburettor float-chamber. If this leaks, the fuel level is reduced and the pump must first supply enough fuel to restore the correct level before a start can be made.

Pump pressure is controlled, in the first instance, by the diaphragm spring. Thus carburettor flooding which sets in when the pump has not been disturbed indicates that the fault lies in the float chamber. However in such a case, if it is persistent, the delivery pressure can be adjusted to help matters by fitting one or two extra gaskets of normal thickness at the pump to crankcase joint. Obviously this packing out must not be carried to excess or high-speed starvation will result.

Excessive wear on the pump itself can normally be due only to poor lubrication, most likely on old engines. The obvious remedy here is, of course, to overhaul the engine.

CARBURETTOR ADJUSTMENTS

On the Solex carburettor only *two* adjustments are possible—setting the slow-running and setting the fast-idling. All other maintenance work is basically cleaning, apart from attention to "mechanical" faults such as an errant automatic choke or a punctured float.

Slow Running Adjustment. This is the adjustment for normal slow running, i.e. with the engine running at working temperature.

KEY TO FIG. 61

1. Bi-metal spring (large) operating choke-valve
2. Bi-metal spring (small) operating stepped cam (7)
3. Vacuum feed passage for heated air drawn from "U" tube (10)
4. Vacuum-kick piston
5. Choke-valve spindle
6. Link and lever connecting vacuum-kick piston (4) and choke-valve spindle (5)
7. Stepped cam
8. Lever for opening throttle for fast idling, or to open choke valve, when partly closed, if accelerator is moved half-way or beyond
9. Hot-air feed pipe from "U" tube (10)
10. "U" tube heated by exhaust gases.
11. Exhaust manifold
12. Choke (strangler) valve
13. Air-correction jet and emulsion tube (B30 PIHT carb)
13A. Air-correction jet and emulsion tube (B30 PIHT-2 carb)
13B. Air correction jet and emulsion tube (B30 PIHT-3 carb)
14. Slow-running jet air-bleed
15. Cold-air feed to "U" tube (10)
16. Slow-running (pilot) jet
17. Float needle-valve and seating
18. Float lever arm (B30 PIHT carb)
19. Choke tube (venturi)
20. Econostat jet
21. Econostat discharge tube
22. Accelerator pump injector tube
23. Accelerator pump discharge valve
24. Accelerator pump diaphragm and plunger
25. Actuating lever
26. Diaphragm return-spring
27. Accelerator pump non-return valve
28. Internal passages in carburettor body
29. Float (B30 PIHT carb)
29A. Float (B30 PIHT-2, B30 PIHT-3 carbs)
30. Main well
31. Main well ball-valve (B3 PIHT carb)
32. Main jet and holder
33. Slow-running mixture volume-control screw
34. Slow-running mixture outlet
35. By-pass orifice (progression hole)
36. Throttle
37. Main spraying orifice
38. Air-correction jet and emulsion tube
39. Main jet
40. Main jet cover-plug

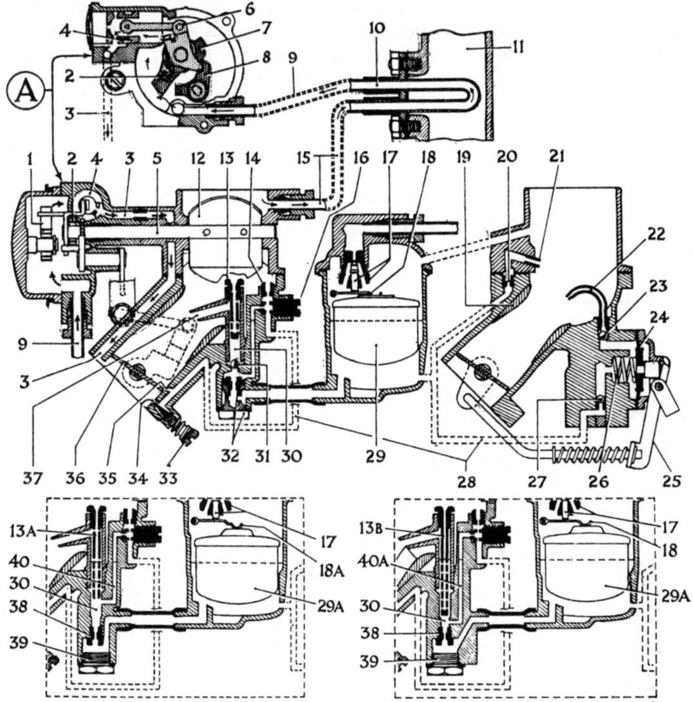

Fig. 61. The Solex Carburettor (Sectional Drawings)

These drawings clearly illustrate the positions of the various carburettor components (*see* also Fig. 62). The three upper drawings apply to the Solex type B30 PIHT carburettor. The two bottom drawings show small differences between part of this instrument and (*left*) the same part of the type B30 PIHT–2 carburettor, and (*right*) the same part of the type B30 PIHT–3 carburettor. "A" is a cross section and end view of the automatic-choke mechanism. The arrows indicate the cold air flow into the "U" tube (*10*) and the hot air flow thence through the automatic-choke mechanism into the inlet manifold.

(*See page* 78 *for Key*)

Consequently this should only be done when the engine has been well warmed up. Adjust as described below.

Screw the slow-running speed adjustment screw (set vertically on the throttle arm) in or out to vary the speed. Turning the screw downwards increases the speed, and screwing it out decreases it. The recommended speed to obtain is 750 r.p.m.—a fast idle.

Now unscrew the slow-running mixture volume-control screw, which you will find next to the carburettor base flange on the side further from the engine, just forward of the vacuum pipe take-off. Loosen this slowly, listening to the engine note. When the unit starts to "hunt" (to surge and run lumpily), turn the screw in the other direction until smooth running is again obtained.

If your engine speed is now too high, slow it down by releasing the speed adjustment screw slightly. If this, in turn, causes the engine to "hunt" make a final small adjustment by screwing in the volume-control screw just a little more until it ceases. Your slow-running adjustment is now correct.

KEY TO FIG. 62

1. Choke-valve spindle and return spring (manual choke)
2. Connecting link for choke to throttle
3. Manual-choke linkage and cable bracket
4. Choke-valve fixing screws and spring washers
5. Choke valve
6. Fixing screw for top body and float-chamber cover
7. Top body and float-chamber cover
8. Float needle-valve assembly and washer
9. Fixing collar and screws
10. Bi-metal spring cover
11. Bi-metal spring (large)
12. Spring clip
13. Choke-valve spindle (automatic choke)
14. Bi-metal spring (small)
15. Strangler valve spindle-bearing bush
16. Fast-idling-lever stepped cam
17. Fast-idling short lever, fixing nut and washer
18. Automatic choke body fixing screws and spring washers
19. Automatic-choke body
20. Vacuum-piston link end (connected to hole in lever on end of (*13*))
21. Set-screw for fast idling adjustment
22. Circlip
23. Fast-idling long lever and spindle
24. Fast-idling connecting-rod pivot
25. Fuel inlet pipe, olive and union nut
26. Gasket (between float chamber and top body)
27. Float lever pivot-pin
28. Retaining spring (float lever pivot-pin)
29. Float lever arm (B30 PIHT, PIHT–3 carbs)
29*A*. Float lever arm (B30 PIHT–2 carb)
30. Float (B30 PIHT carb)
30*A*. Float (B30 PIHT–2, B30 PIHT–3 carbs)
31. Float chamber
32. Accelerator-pump lever operating-spring
33. Circlip
34. Accelerator-pump operating rod
35. Nut (accelerator-pump lever)
36 Accelerator-pump lever
37. Spacing washer

38. Gasket (between carburettor top body and main body)
39. Emulsion tube and air-correction jet (B30 PIHT carb)
39*A*. Emulsion tube and air-correction jet (B30 PIHT–2 carb)
39*B*. Emulsion tube and air-correction jet (B30 PIHT–3 carb)
40. Ball valve for main well (B30 PIHT carb)
41. Pilot jet air-bleed
42. Econostat jet
43. Carburettor main body
43*A*. Carburettor main body ·difference (B30 PIHT–2, B30 PIHT–3 carbs)
44. Plastic tube (float chamber to main body)
45. Pilot jet (slow-running)
46. Accelerator-pump diaphragm return-spring
47. Accelerator-pump diaphragm
48. Accelerator-pump body
49. Cover fixing-screw (short)
50. Accelerator pump pivot-pin
51. Accelerator-pump lever
52. Cover fixing-screw (long)
53. Slow-running volume-control screw
54. Volume-control screw spring
55. Main jet holder (B30 PIHT carb)
55*A*. Main jet cover-plug
56. Main jet holder or cover-plug washer
57. Main jet (B30 PIHT carb)
57*A*. Main jet (B30 PIHT–2, B30 PIHT–3 carbs)
58. Choke tube (B30 PIHT and B30 PIHT–2 carbs)
58*A*. Choke tube (B30 PIHT–3 carb)
59. Choke tube locating-screw and locking washer
60. Throttle valve
61. Throttle-valve fixing screws
62. Throttle spindle
63. Slow-running adjustment screw and spring
64. Fast-idling linkage (B30 PIHT carb)
65. Fast-idling linkage (B30 PIHT–2, B30 PIHT–3 carbs)
66. Fast-idling linkage (manual choke carb)

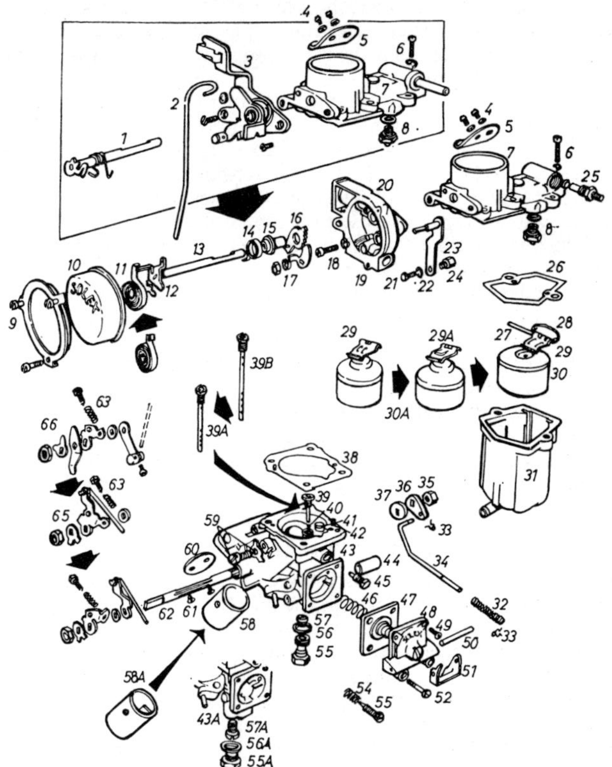

FIG. 62. EXPLODED VIEW OF SOLEX CARBURETTOR

When stripping the carburettor, refer to this detailed drawing (*see* also Fig. 61) for the positions of the various parts in relation to each other. Numerals with the suffix *A* and *B* apply to type B30 PIHT–2 and B30 PIHT–3 carburettors respectively.

(*See page 80 for Key*)

Fast-idling Adjustment. For setting the fast-idling adjustment you will have to remove the carburettor. Depending on the model this involves: releasing the throttle air pipe or loosening the cable clamp and freeing the control cable; detaching the fuel line; detaching the vacuum pipe; removing the air filter; and taking off the two nuts which hold the carburettor and its associated base-plate in position. The unit can then be lifted off, complete with the two pipes to the automatic choke, which are merely a push fit in the exhaust "U" tube.

Remove the three screws which hold the black cover of the automatic choke and take it off. Then, referring to Fig. 61, open the throttle, slip a rubber band round the stepped cam (*7*) and turn it so that it can be held by the band in its highest position.

At the base of the cranked lever which hangs down from the rear face of the automatic choke is a set-screw. This clamps the short rod which connects the choke lever to the throttle arm. This mechanism actuates the short lever (*8*) in the choke. Loosen the set-bolt, and open the throttle to give the fast-idling setting of 0·029 in. This seemingly obscure measurement is easy to arrange; just insert the shank of a No. 69 drill between the edge of the throttle butterfly and the carburettor bore, at right angles to the spindle. Now tighten up the set-bolt again.

This completes the fast-idling adjustment, but check that when the short lever (*8*) is resting against the top step of the cam (*7*) the throttle is in fact open by the correct amount. To do this, use the drill shank as you would a feeler gauge. You can, of course, use feelers instead if you wish.

When replacing the automatic-choke cover, note that the end of the bi-metal spring engages with the peg projecting from the vacuum-kick lever (*6*). The cover must then be turned until the line which is scribed on its edge mates with the notch on the casting just forward of the vacuum-kick piston housing. Then tighten the screws, and refit the carburettor.

CARBURETTOR MAINTENANCE

Cleaning the Carburettor. This job can be done without removing the instrument from the car. Take off the air filter and clean away any road dirt with rag. Then, referring to Fig. 61, remove the main jet and holder (*32*) or the main jet cover-plug (*40*), using a $\frac{9}{16}$ in. A/F box spanner. This drains the float chamber and the slow running system passageway, and by operating the fuel pump priming lever a jet of fuel can be spurted through to clean the needle valve and also its seating.

Now use a small screwdriver to detach the main jet from its holder or, in the case of the later carburettor, the main jet (*39*) from the carburettor body. From the side of the instrument remove the slow-running (pilot) jet (*16*). Blow through both jets and then inspect their orifices to ensure that the jets are clear. If they are, replace them and refit the main-jet plug.

On top of the float chamber are two screws. Remove these, and you will find that you can draw the float chamber downwards and forwards to free it from the carburettor body. It comes away complete with its float. You can lift it out once the small spring which locks its fulcrum pin in place has been eased out of the slot. Then clean out the float chamber and inspect the float for damage. When reassembling, note that the float fulcrum-lever (*18, 42*) has the word "Top" stamped on it to ensure that it goes back the right way round. Correct replacement is important.

Refit the float chamber, making sure that it seats properly against its joint washer in the carburettor top body and that it engages correctly with the short plastic tube which connects it to the float chamber. Set a mirror under the instrument and inspect the chamber/tube/body joints for leakage when the fuel pump priming lever is operated to fill the float chamber.

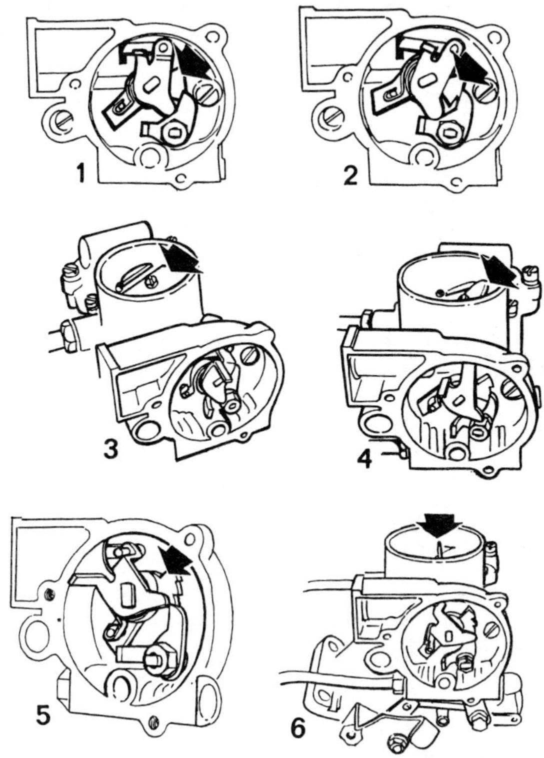

FIG. 63A. OPERATION OF THE AUTOMATIC CHOKE

1, the fast idle stepped cam in moderate cold starting position; 2, fast idle stepped cam in very cold starting position; 3, choke valve in cold starting position, all conditions; 4, auto choke and choke valve immediately after starting; 5, fast idle stepped cam in normal hot running position; 6, choke valve in hot running position.

To drain the accelerator pump, loosen the four brass screws which hold it to the main body, and gently draw the diaphragm assembly away from the unit. Afterwards retighten the screws carefully.

The carburettor top body should not be disturbed while the unit is still

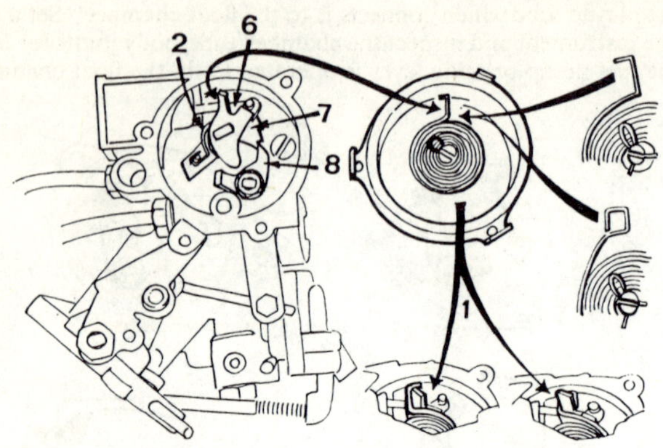

FIG. 63B. AUTOMATIC CHOKE LAYOUT

The insets show differences in the construction and fitting of bi-metal springs. The parts numbered are bi-metal spring for choke valve (1); bi-metal spring for stepped cam (2); vacuum-kick piston/choke valve spindle link (6); stepped cam (7); throttle preset lever (8).

on the car, owing to the difficulty of subsequent refitting. For a complete strip giving access to the rest of the internals—slow-running jet air-bleed; accelerator-pump discharge tube; air-correction jet; econostat jet and discharge tube; and the float-needle assembly, the carburettor must be removed and the dismantling done on the bench (*see* Fig. 62).

Follow the same procedure as for adjustment of the fast-idling, up to the time that the carburettor is detached. Then merely release the screws which secure the top cover, lift it, and pivot it *towards* the accelerator-pump side *without* disconnecting any of the linkage. All the parts just detailed (*see* Fig. 63B) are then readily accessible.

Carburettor Troubles and Their Remedies. If poor performance or excessive fuel consumption is encountered, the carburettor is the last suspect—to be dealt with only after all other possible causes have been checked and eliminated. For poor fuel consumption, examine the whole fuel system for leakage; ensure that the float chamber is not flooding; that the automatic choke is operating properly; that the main jet and its holder or plug are secure; and that both the jets are of the recommended size (*see* page 118 in the Appendix).

For loss of speed, make sure that the throttle is opening properly; that there is no fuel obstruction in the econostat circuit; that the air-filter element is not fouled; and that the pump is delivering an ample supply of fuel.

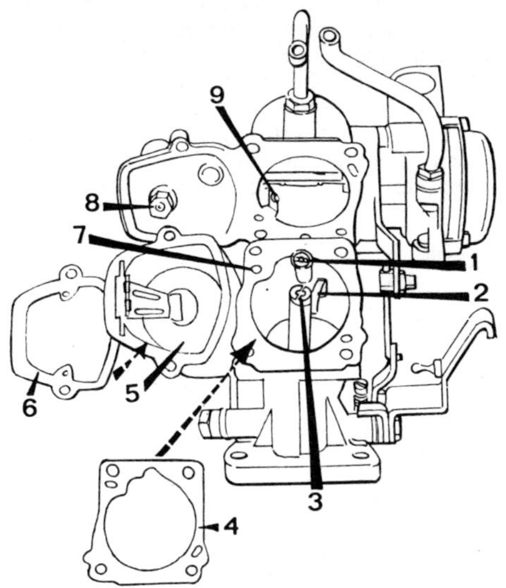

FIG. 63C.

Pivotting the carburettor top on the fast-idle linkage gives access to—

1. Slow-running jet
2. Accelerator-pump discharge tube
3. Air-correction jet
4. Gasket
5. Float
6. Float-chamber gasket
7. Econostat jet
8. Needle-valve assembly
9. Econostat discharge tube

Where the slow-running is faulty, make the check already described, and also detach the slow-running jet to see if it is clear. Make sure that there are no air leaks anywhere in the induction system, and that the volume-control screw is not damaged or its locking spring missing.

Difficult cold starting suggests choke trouble. This may be a result of dirt making the choke spindle stiff; or it could be that the cover of the choke has not been properly fitted. Check this point. Referring to Fig. 62, two different types of bi-metal spring (11) have been used—one with a looped end; the other without. When fitting a cover with the former type of spring, the looped end must fit over the lever on the strangler spindle (12) and the cover must then be turned to match the scribed line and notch as described on page 82. With the unlooped spring, the cover is first set with the line in the 9 o'clock position and it is then rotated until the line and notch coincide.

To remedy a "flat spot" occurring at small throttle openings, first test the induction system for air leaks and ensure that the vacuum pipe is fitted correctly and is not fractured or punctured. Examine the by-pass orifice (*35*) for blockage. If these three tests give no positive results it is just possible that the diaphragm in the vacuum advance-retard mechanism (on the distributor) is faulty, although this is a rare complaint.

Poor acceleration suggests an accelerator-pump defect. Check its action by removing the air filter and watching what happens when the throttle arm is jerked open. Fuel should spurt from the accelerator-pump discharge tube. If the flow is not copious, or no fuel at all is ejected, the

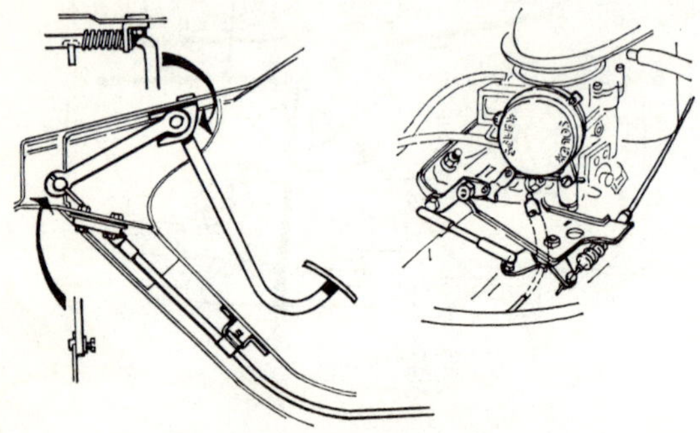

FIG. 64. THE CABLE-OPERATED THROTTLE

Replacing the unsatisfactory pneumatic throttle-control, a cable is now routed through the channel in the centre of the floor pan. The front attachment is by a solderless nipple to the lever on the accelerator pedal spindle. This is hidden inside a cover on the bulkhead, which is merely bolted down. The attachment at the carburettor end is also by a solderless nipple. To change a cable, remove the inner cover and free both cable nipples. Pull out the old inner cable, lubricate the new one, and feed it into the original outer casing from the carburettor end.

pump's ball valves (*23*, *27*) may be clogged with dirt. A previous owner may even have omitted to replace them after stripping the carburettor. Another possible assembly fault which could have the same result is incorrect replacement of the pump's diaphragm spring (*26*).

Manual Choke Carburettors. Where these are fitted, they are identical to the Solex B30 PIHT–2 instruments except for the float-chamber top and the choke mechanism. Servicing procedure is the same except that the auto-choke instructions are not applicable.

STROMBERG CD CARBURETTOR

The constant-vacuum Stromberg carburettor is of basically simple design and is almost foolproof in operation. In fact, the commonest trouble is that some previous owner may have toyed with the jets and needles, and so upset the balance. The correct jet for the 125 CDS unit is the 0·090 in. An 0·100 in.

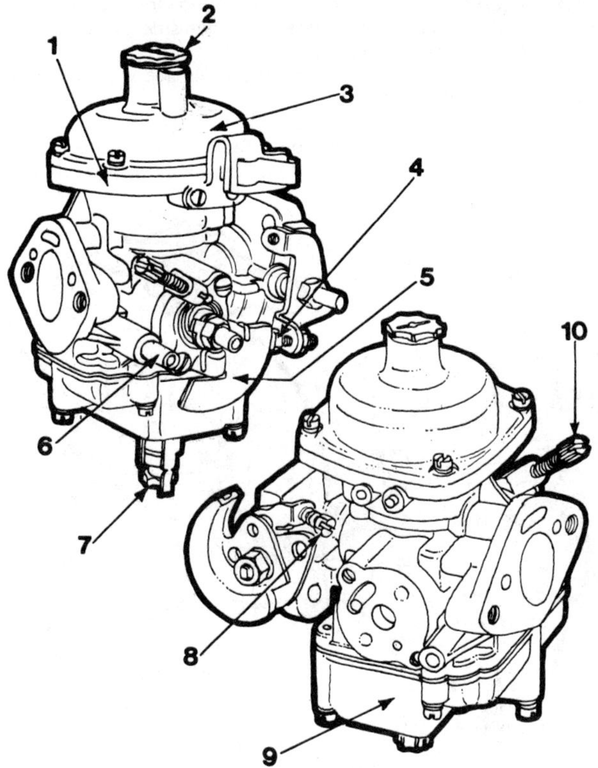

FIG. 65. THE ZENITH-STROMBERG 125 CD CARBURETTOR, EXTERNAL

1, Body; 2, Air valve hydraulic damper; 3, Depression chamber cover; 4, Cold fast-idle speed adjustment; 5, Fast-idle cam; 6, Fuel inlet; 7, Jet adjustment; 8, Slow-running adjuster screw; 9, Float chamber; 10, Starter assembly travel adjustment.

jet is used in the 175 CD instrument. For use below 5,000 ft. the metering needle should be a 6K (B.17351Z). For use in areas between 5,000 and 10,000 ft. a 5U (B.17751Z) needle is required, and above 10,000 ft. the standard fitting is a 5V (B.17752Z).

In cases of uneven running, then, first check that the jet and needle are standard. Both have their numbers embossed upon them.

Slow-running adjustment. This is done in the following stages:

1 Unbolt the oil cooler and move it to one side to ease access. Be careful not to strain the pipes.
2 Remove the air cleaner assembly and detach the two air intake elbows from the carburettors.
3 Screw up each jet-adjusting nut (at the base of the carburettor) until the jet just contacts the lower face of the air valve piston, but does not raise it. This is best "felt" by removing the top plug that

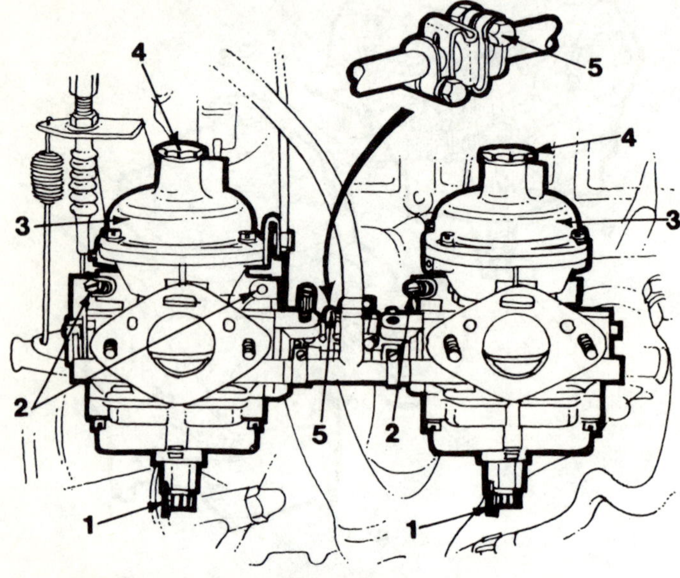

FIG. 66. ADJUSTMENT, THROTTLE SYNCHRONIZATION AND JETS

1, Jet adjustment; 2, Slow-running adjuster screws; 3, Depression chamber; 4, Air valve hydraulic damper; 5, Bolt, flexible coupling.

carries the hydraulic valve damper, and inserting a screwdriver to rest on the piston. With gentle pressure on the screwdriver, you can sense the moment that the jet and piston touch.

4 Now check that the piston can move freely. Insert a finger to lift the piston and then let it fall. It should drop back into place. Repeat all operations with the second carburettor.
5 Next, slacken the jet adjusting screws on *both* carburettors by two complete turns. A small coin makes a useful "screwdriver" here.
6 Top up the damper bores with oil. A special oil for this purpose is

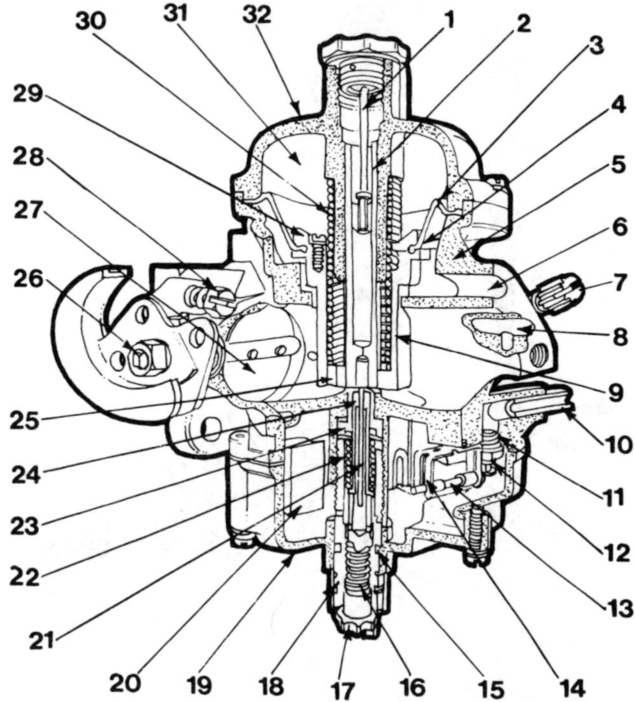

FIG. 67. ZENITH-STROMBERG 125 CD—SECTIONED VIEW

1, Air valve piston hydraulic damper; 2, Guide; 3, Diaphragm; 4, Air chamber; 5, Body; 6, Air feed hole to air chamber; 7, Starter assembly travel adjustment; 8, Float chamber air feed; 9, Air valve piston; 10, Fuel inlet; 11, Jet centralizing bush; 12, Float needle valve and seat; 13, Float fulcrum pin; 14, Float fulcrum; 15, 16, O-rings; 17, Jet adjustment; 18, Jet bush retaining screw; 19, Float chamber; 20, Float; 21, Metering needle; 22, Jet spring; 23, O-ring; 24, Jet; 25, Depression transfer hole; 26, Spindle; 27, Throttle valve; 28, Slow-running speed adjuster; 29, Diaphragm retainer ring; 30, Piston return spring; 31, Depression chamber; 32, Chamber cover.

produced by Zenith (the makers of the carburettor) and this should be used as a matter of course.

7 A flexible coupling links the throttles of the twin carburettors. Release its coupling bolt, and then unscrew both slow-speed running adjustment screws on the throttles until their ends clear their abutments. The head of the stop bolt that bears on the fast-idle cam at the point nearest the manifold must also be screwed inwards so that it comes clear, allowing the throttles to close.

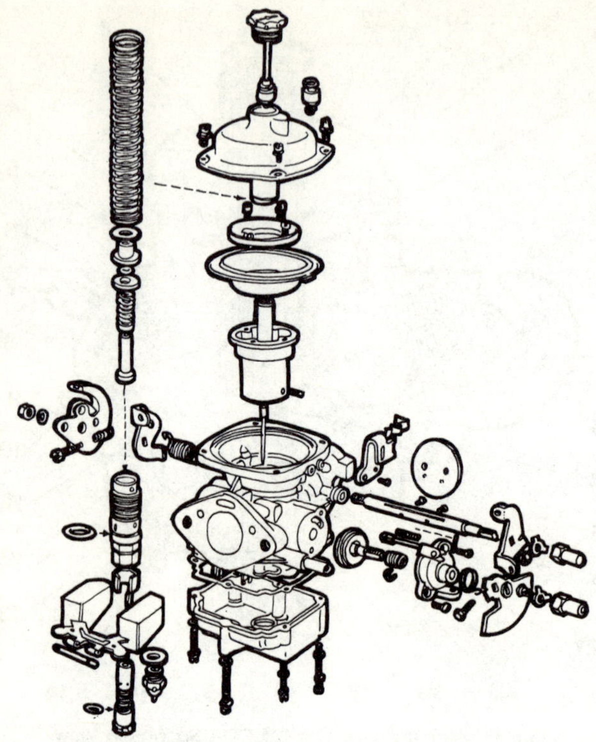

FIG. 68. THE ZENITH-STROMBERG 125 CD CARBURETTOR "EXPLODED"

Make sure that both have done so. Then retighten the flexible coupling bolt.

8 Hold each throttle in turn fully closed, and screw up the appropriate slow-running adjustment screw till it just touches its abutment. Then give it exactly $1\frac{1}{4}$ more turns clockwise.

9 Start the engine and run it until it reaches normal operating temperature.

10 By turning each adjusting screw *an equal amount*, set the idling speed to 1,000 r.p.m. on the tachometer.

11 To improve the idling, it is permissible to reset the jet adjustment screws by no more than a quarter of a turn up or down. Clockwise movement weakens the mixture. Turning anti-clockwise enriches it.

12 Use a length of rubber tubing to listen to the hiss at each intake. Both carburettors should make the same sound. Imbalance can be corrected by loosening the flexible coupling and adjusting one throttle independently. When the same sound is audible from both, retighten the coupling.

13 Once the idling is satisfactory, reset the clearance between the bolt head and the cam to 0·012 in.

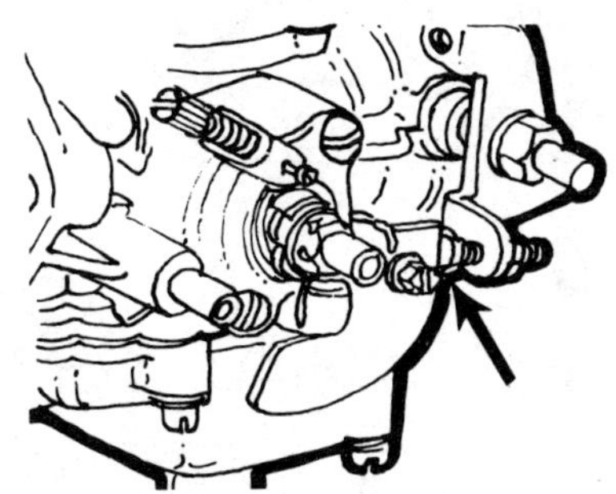

FIG. 69. COLD STARTING SYNCHRONIZATION

With the choke control fully home, there must be 0·012 in. clearance between the bolt head (arrowed) and the fast-idle cam.

14 Replace the intake elbows and the air cleaner, and bolt the oil cooler back into place.

Starter assembly. If the carburettors have been removed and separated the interconnection between the starter assemblies will have to be reset. The sequence is:

1 First, the clamping bolt on one of the interconnections must be released.

2 Ensure that the choke control is properly adjusted and is as far down as possible. When this requirement is met, the cam on the rear carburettor will be resting against its back stop on the carburettor body.

3 Check that the cam on the front instrument is also against its stop. Then reconnect the coupling bolt.

4 Note that there is an alternative position for the starter assembly stop. Normally, the cross-peg on the stop lies over the slot in the body abutment. For very cold conditions (below −23° C. or −10° F.) the stop can be pressed inwards and turned through 90°. This allows the peg to engage in the slot. In this position, an extra-rich mixture is supplied for starting.

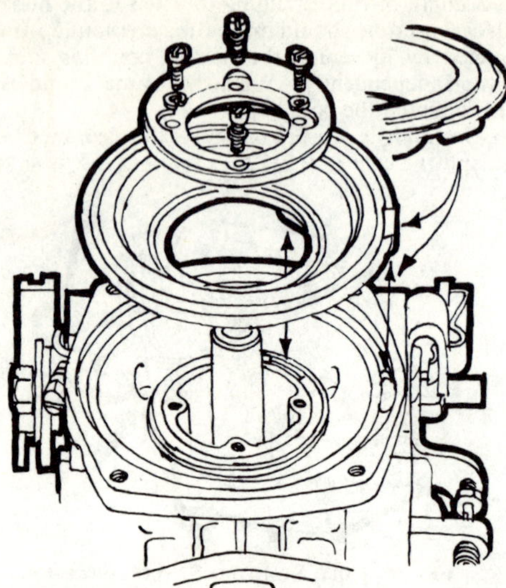

Fig. 70. Diaphragm Location

When refitting a diaphragm, ensure that the projections in its face engage in the slots
shown here.

Diaphragm removal. In time, the diaphragm in the depression chamber
may deteriorate. Renewal can be carried out without removing the
carburettors, thus:

    1 Undo the four screws holding the depression chamber cover.

    2 Lift out the air valve piston.

    3 Undo the four screws holding the diaphragm retaining ring.

    4 Detach the old diaphragm and offer up the replacement, ensuring
that the locating tabs engage in the slots in the body and in the
upper end of the air valve piston.

    5 Taking care not to displace the diaphragm, refit the retaining ring
and replace the cover.

Cleaning the Stromberg. To do this work properly it is essential to
remove the carburettors from the engine. When this has been done, wash
the exteriors thoroughly to get rid of all dirt before the instruments are
opened up. Then:

    1 Six screws hold the float chamber. Release them and pull the
chamber downwards. It has to ride off over the O-ring seal on the
jet bushing retaining screw, and this is a very tight fit. Quite a
sharp tug may be needed to pull the float chamber clear.

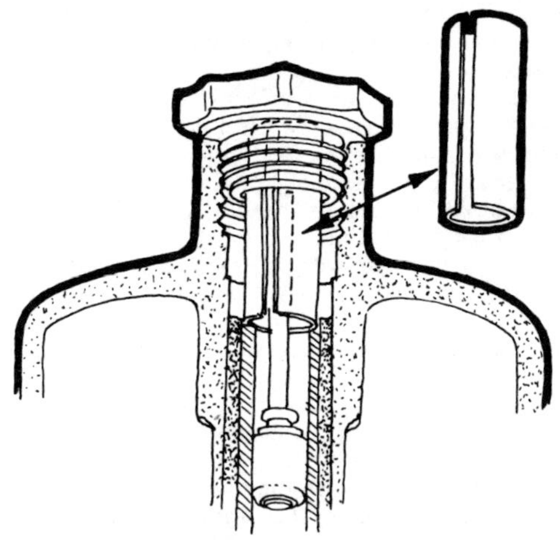

FIG. 71. AIR VALVE PISTON STOP

This simple tool can be made up to aid holding down the piston while adjustments are made to the jet position. It is a section of copper tube, $1\frac{5}{32}$–$1\frac{3}{16}$ in. long. Its maximum outside diameter is 0·49 in. and the inside diameter 0·38 in. Slot it to clear the damper rod.

2 Unclip the float and shake it to check whether it has been punctured. If it has you will hear petrol swill around inside.

3 With a thin-walled box spanner, unscrew the needle valve assembly. Remember that if this is done a new washer *must* be used on reassembly. Service kits provide a choice of three. The one to use is whichever is the same thickness as the original.

4 The air valve piston, needle and diaphragm should be lifted out.

5 Blow through the fuel feed hole in the float chamber and, at the same time, move the starter assembly over its whole range of movement several times. The travel stop must be in its "out" position while this is being done.

6 Use petrol or paraffin to clean the internals. Nothing else is permissible, since some cleaning and degreasing fluids can attack the diaphragm and O-rings. There is no need to remove the jet bush retaining screw when cleaning. However, if you wish to renew the O-rings undo the screw and remove the holder. Then undo the adjuster (the lowest screw) and slip out the jet.

7 Check that the metering needle's shoulder is exactly flush with the face of the piston. It can be adjusted after loosening the grub screw on the side of the piston.

8 Screw in the jet assembly finger tight. Screw the adjuster fully home, then loosen it by two and a half turns.

9 Refit the air valve piston, diaphragm and cover, and the float assembly.

10 Slacken the jet assembly by a full turn, lift the air valve piston, and press it down with a screwdriver inserted through the damper hole. This will centralize the needle.

11 Tighten the jet assembly. To ensure that the needle remains centralized, it is best to keep lifting and dropping the piston while the jet is tightened up.

12 Top up the damper with oil, and refit the carburettors. Then carry out the adjusting and synchronizing sequence already described.

Renewing air filter elements. Having disconnected the flame trap hose from the air intake tube, release the four spring clips that hold the upper body to the lower. If these clips are stiff, the job can be eased by pressing down on the top cover with the flat of the hand. Both elements can be lifted out when the cover is off.

If the job is being done with the filter body in place, take care not to allow any trapped dirt to enter the carburettors while the lower section is being cleaned. Once both sections have been freed of dirt, fit new rubber sealing rings and two new elements, closed sides upwards. Refit the upper body, making sure the clips snap securely into place, and refit the hose.

9 Steering, suspension, wheels

MEDDLING unnecessarily with vital components such as those on the steering and suspension is one thing, conscientious maintenance is quite another. The one is potentially, even criminally, dangerous while the other is essential if the inherent safety of the car is to be preserved. This chapter is therefore deliberately restricted, and all work which is not easily within the compass of an ordinary motorist equipped with a reasonable tool kit has been omitted.

THE STEERING

Steering Maintenance. The steering rack is a sealed unit, and lubrication is not required unless the rack has been stripped. There is no provision for routine adjustment, and maintenance is restricted to keeping the fixing nuts tight and ensuring that there is no leakage of oil.

The fixing nuts (*see* Fig. 72) are located beneath the car (two on each

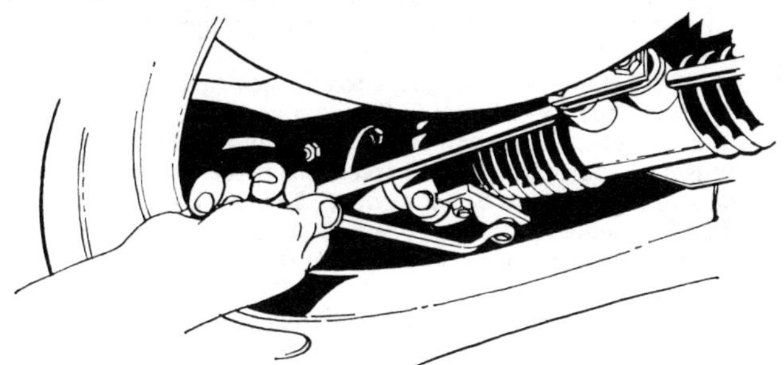

FIG. 72. TIGHTENING THE NUTS ON THE STEERING RACK "U" BOLTS

The security of the "U" bolts and nuts which hold the steering rack in place is a vital check to make. Ideally the nuts should be tightened to the correct torque, but in the absence of a torque wrench tighten them so that they are really tight when normal hand pressure is exerted with a standard-length spanner.

side of the rack) on the "U" bolts holding the rack to the support bracket. They should be torqued to 16 lb ft.

Oil Leakage from Steering Rack. Where a persistent leakage is discovered, the steering rack should be removed from the car and the fault rectified. Nothing can be done with it still in position. This work is best entrusted to a qualified Chrysler agent.

Steering Alignment. Of the two track rods, only the off-side one is adjustable and it is this which is attended to when the steering has to be re-aligned. The correct "toe-in" is $\frac{3}{16}$ in. Although this is the average recommended, a "toe-in" between $\frac{1}{16}$ in. and $\frac{5}{16}$ in. is permissible. It is better not to attempt steering realignment at home, but to have the car checked at a service garage with professional equipment which is accurate to within fractions of a degree.

Damper Adjustment. Set in the body of the steering rack is a screw which controls the damper unit. This is intended as a means of taking up end float when the rack is on the bench. It is *not* an adjustment which should be made with the rack still in the car.

The recommended method of adjusting the damper is to use a dial test-indicator. With the stylus of the indicator on the control screw, it should be slackened to give 0·003 in. damper pad end-float at the tightest point along the stroke of the rack, after the screw has first been tightened enough for its nose to contact the centre of the plastic damper.

Track-rod Joints. Where a track-rod joint has developed serious play, it must be renewed. You can test for play by blocking up the front of the car and attempting alternately to pull the wheels together and then push them apart.

Release the locking plate on the steering rack (a new one is required for reassembly) and detach the ball-joint nut. Hold a heavy hammer against the ball-joint housing on the track rod and strike the opposite side of the housing a sharp blow with a second hammer. This will release the taper and allow the joint to be withdrawn. The new components can then be fitted and the nuts tightened. The ball-joint nut is torqued to 33 lb ft and the track rod/steering-unit nut to 53 lb ft.

Steering Troubles. Where no excessive play is obvious in either the action of the rack or in the ball joints, steering troubles are likely to be rooted in the tyres or wheels.

THE TYRES AND WHEELS

Tyre Pressures. Correct inflation of all four tyres is *vital*. Owing to the pronounced rear-end bias, the rear tyres must be kept inflated to approximately *double* the pressure of the front tyres. If they are not, the stability of the car seriously deteriorates. For example, I have driven an Imp on which some homicidal maniac in a dealer's workshop had switched the front and rear wheels over without subsequently adjusting the tyre pressures. The result was fantastic. At 30 m.p.h. the front end of the car constantly swung from one side to another and steering correction proved useless.

The above is an extreme case, but it illustrates well the necessity for sticking to the recommended pressures of 15 lb for the front tyres and 30 lb per sq in. for the rear tyres. At the cost of a harder ride and an increase in body noise, however, these pressures can be increased by 5 lb per sq in., resulting in slightly better steering. To avoid unnecessary tyre wear, check their pressures *weekly*. Also change over the wheels about every 5,000 miles (*see* Fig. 73).

At the first sign of any tendency for the car to wander, the tyre pressures should be checked. If these are correct, the balance of the wheels should also be checked. This is best done on a garage's wheel-balancing machine.

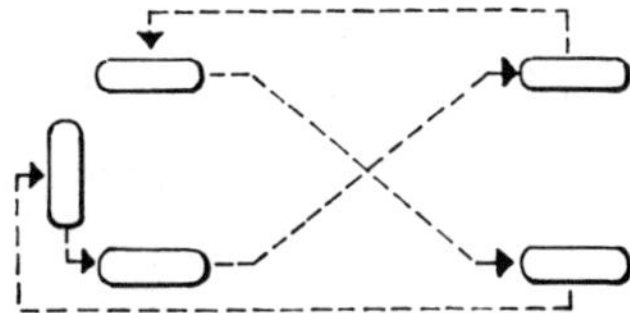

FIG. 73. CHANGE THE WHEELS ROUND LIKE THIS EVERY 5,000 MILES

The effect of changing the wheels round as indicated is to even out wear on the tyre treads. When doing this remember to adjust the tyre pressures accordingly (*see* text), otherwise the handling of the car will be badly upset. When tyre renewal becomes necessary, see that all four tyres are of the same make and type.

The cost, with weights, is usually about 50p per wheel. As properly balanced wheels not only improve the car's handling but also lengthen tyre life, this is a good investment.

The Wheel and Hub Nuts. The security of the wheel nuts is, of course, another important consideration. These nuts should all be torqued to 48 lb ft. Yet another culprit (one which is all too easy to overlook) is the rear hub-securing-nut (*see* Fig. 75). This nut is locked by a tab-washer of substantial size, but I have personally seen a case in which this nut was in fact loose even though the washer, on close inspection, seemed tight and intact.

To check for wheel slackness, jack up the car and, having removed the wheel disc, try rocking each wheel. If there is perceptible movement it means that either the wheel securing-nuts or the hub securing nut (and lock-nut also on a front hub) are loose.

The rear hub securing nut should be torqued to 170 lb ft—well beyond the range of most torque wrenches. However, to tighten this large nut satisfactorily a long ring spanner can be used, and adequate tension can be ensured quite simply. All you need to do is to tighten the nut as tightly as possible by hand. Then set the ring spanner just above the horizontal and *stand on it*. You know your own weight. If it happens to be 170 lb. you should stand at a point one foot from the centre of the spanner. That will then give a load of 170 lb ft. Heavyweights should stand a little closer; lighter folk a little farther out! Make sure that your whole weight is applied. Do not hold on to the car, as this will obviously take a proportion of your weight off the spanner. The lock-nut for the front hub bearing-adjuster nut (*see* Fig. 74) should be torqued to 13 lb ft.

Where everything else is in order, bad steering can be due to wheel rim damage or to worn hub bearings. The rim should have a maximum "run out" of $\frac{3}{32}$ in. Greater distortion than this means you have a buckled wheel which should be discarded at once.

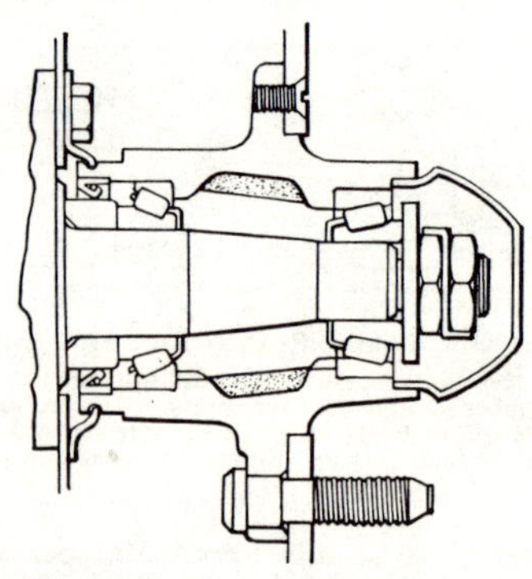

FIG. 74. SHOWING THE FRONT-HUB ROLLER BEARINGS (ADJUSTABLE)

This drawing of a section through the front hub shows (shaded) the extent to which grease should be packed in after cleaning. Grease the adjustable roller bearings also, but do not fill the hub cap, otherwise grease may get on the brake-shoe linings and reduce braking power.

Hub Bearing Adjustment. Only the hub bearings for the *front* wheels can be adjusted. These are of the taper-roller type (*see* Fig. 74), and the correct procedure, if bearing slackness develops, should always be followed when adjusting them. The ball bearings in the rear wheel hubs have no adjustment (*see* Fig. 75). To adjust the roller bearings of a front-wheel hub, proceed as follows.

First jack the car up so that the front wheel concerned is clear of the ground. Then, referring to Fig. 74, release the tab-washer holding the lock-nut and remove both this nut and the washer. Behind the washer is the roller bearing adjuster-nut. This should be tightened to a torque of 4–5 lb ft while simultaneously spinning the front wheel. Then loosen the adjuster nut by 2½ to 3 flats (not *turns*) and remove the torque spanner. Replace the tab-washer and lock-nut and tighten the latter to 13 lb ft.

Where new roller bearings have been fitted, the end float should then be measured and should fall within the limits 0·003 in.–0·0065 in. If this reading is not obtained, the adjustment should be repeated.

Lubrication of Front Hubs. The front wheel hubs are lubricated with grease and when lubrication is required (seldom) each hub should be removed and dismantled for repacking with grease. After jacking up the car and removing the wheel, detach the brake drum. This is done by slackening off the brake-shoe adjustment and removing the countersunk screw which secures the brake drum. Then prise off the hub cap. Note

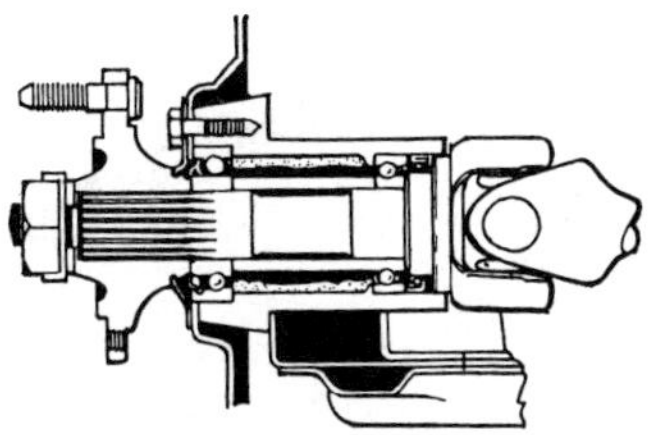

FIG. 75. SHOWING THE REAR-HUB BEARINGS (NON-ADJUSTABLE)

No adjustment is necessary or provided, and the lubricant is sealed-in for the duration of the rear bearings. To renew them, first remove the centre nut and draw off the flange. Next detach the drive shaft and drift out the old bearings. Then grease the new bearings, insert them, and fill the area shown shaded above with fresh grease of the recommended grade and type.

that on the near-side wheel this covers the speedometer-drive cam which must also be detached.

Now remove the tab-washer, lock-nut, bearing adjuster-nut, and "D" washer, and pull the hub off the front stub-axle. Take out the inner cone of the outer roller-bearing, prise out the grease seal, and remove the inner cone from the other bearing. Wash the hub and both inner cones in petrol, taking care not to mix them up, and allow them to drain completely dry.

Examine the roller bearings for any signs of damage. Pitting on their races means that replacement is *essential*. Where this is necessary, the outer tracks can be drifted from the housing.

Whether the old bearings are refitted or new ones used, they must be packed with grease of the recommended grade (*see* page 116) before use. Grease should be packed into each inner bearing, and also into the interior of the hub. It should just fill the recess in the hub inner face. Beware of overpacking with grease, for the excess will melt and find its way on to the brake-shoe linings.

Check that grease has not cut a groove in the stub-axle distance-piece;

if it has, this must be chiselled off and a new part pressed on. To re-assemble the hub, follow in the reverse order the instructions already given for dismantling it.

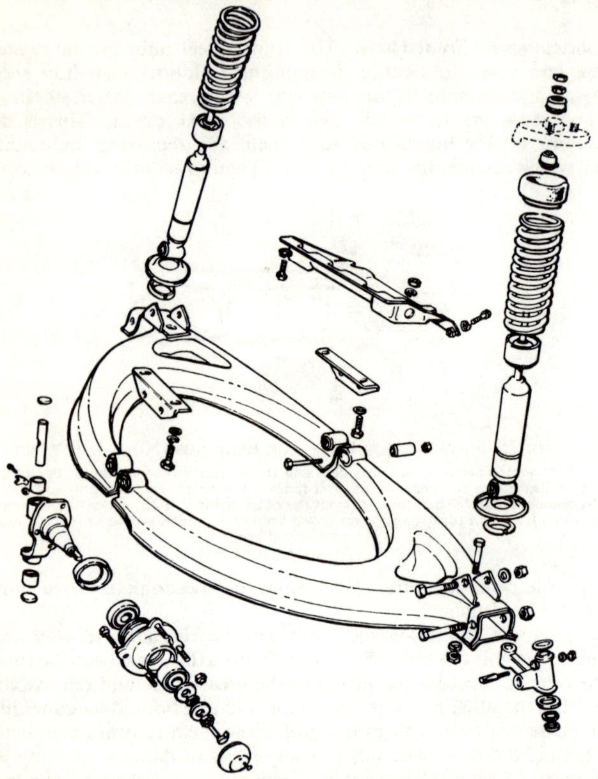

FIG. 76. EXPLODED VIEW SHOWING DETAILS OF THE IMP FRONT SUSPENSION

The Imp's swinging-axle front suspension has no grease points, except on the king-pins on later models, and the hub bearings require only occasional cleaning and packing with fresh grease (*see* Fig. 74). Check all pivots regularly for security.

Note that the front hub caps must not be greased. This is essential, and do not mix up the two caps. The near-side one has a small peg which drives the speedometer cam. The off-side one is plain.

THE SUSPENSION

Front Suspension Check. Only eight pivot points (*see* Fig. 76) need examination—two on each of the "wishbones," and two on each damper. The "wishbone" pivots comprise through-bolts secured by nuts with Nylon inserts, passing through metal and rubber-bonded bushes. They should be torqued to 25 lb ft. If the through-bolts are removed for any reason, the nuts may be used again, so long as their threads are in good order and the inserts have not lost their locking properties.

The shock-absorber is secured by a through-bolt at its lower end (torque, 43 lb ft) and by a central stud and nuts to the upper bracket. There should be no perceptible play in any of these joints.

If, on testing the front suspension pivots (with the car jacked up), play is discovered, the "wishbone(s)" must be removed. This is a job best left to an agent. This applies also to the removal of the front suspension dampers which likewise entails releasing the front springs. For this, a garage jack is a necessity, an item of equipment unlikely to be found in the average home workshop.

Rear Suspension Check. At the back of the car there is nothing to attend to except to examine the pivot points for security at least once a year after making an initial 500 mile check. Using a torque wrench, test the following: cross-member to car body, 27 lb ft; engine mounting to cross-member, 27 lb ft; shock-absorber to car body, 11 lb ft; shock-absorber to suspension, 25 lb ft; suspension pivot-bolts, 48 lb ft.

The Hydraulic Dampers. Bucking on poor road surfaces may have nothing to do with tyre inflation pressures but may point to faulty suspension-spring dampers or to insecure damper mountings. These latter are usually evidenced by a knocking sound when bumps are encountered, or when cornering. Sometimes this is also caused by an insecurely welded damper-attachment on the car bodywork, a fault which can be cured only by spot-welding.

10 The braking system

THIS is the most vital chapter in this book, for the simple reason that the efficiency of the car's braking system is perhaps the most important single consideration in motoring. An inefficient engine is not desirable, but neither is it particularly dangerous. The same cannot be said of an inefficient braking system. Lives depend upon the brakes working well and continuing to work well.

Every job which the private owner can do as well as the professional is dealt with here. But I have not included instructions for stripping and rebuilding hydraulic master and slave cylinders, nor even for renewing brake hoses. The reason is that the risk involved is not, in my opinion, worth the small saving in money which would result from doing this yourself.

Professional mechanics working with fine tools in well-equipped work-shops obviously have an advantage here over the average private owner. The best that he can hope for is to raise the car on ramps on a dusty garage floor and to work on a part-time bench. This is adequate for most of the heavier stuff; but I do not think it good enough for the delicate internals of the hydraulic system.

My advice is: inspect the system regularly and have any incipient faults corrected before they can develop to serious proportions. Attend to all maintenance detailed in this chapter. For the rest, entrust it to a Chrysler dealer.

Check Hydraulic Fluid Level Weekly. Before removing the cap from the master-cylinder reservoir (located at the front, on the off-side) first wipe all round the cap with a piece of clean rag. Do not take the cap off till all dirt has been removed from the area. This is essential. Then detach the cap; place it on a clean piece of paper laid on the floor of the luggage compartment, and add sufficient hydraulic fluid to bring the level in the reservoir up to the top of the internal division. Only clean new fluid should be used. Check the breather holes in the cap and screw it firmly back into place.

The hydraulic fluid level in the system should be checked at regular intervals—certainly at least once a week. Any sudden fall in the level indicates that there is a leak in the system; this must be located and rectified.

Bleeding the Brakes. During operation, air may enter the system and result in a "spongy" feel in the brake pedal. One has to pump the pedal once or twice to obtain positive braking. This is a sure sign that the system should be bled.

You will need a clean jar; some fresh brake fluid; a length of rubber tube having an internal bore small enough to fit closely over the brake bleed nipples; and an assistant to operate the brake pedal.

Before bleeding is tackled, examine all the brake pipes and unions for signs of leakage. Any faults should be corrected first, otherwise you will simply be wàsting your time. Once assured on that point, you can start work, beginning with the left-hand rear cylinder.

Remove the rubber cover from the bleed valve and press the end of your rubber tube over the nipple. Pour some of your fresh hydraulic fluid into the jar and immerse the end of the pipe in it. The pipe must stay immersed throughout the operation, otherwise air will be drawn back into the system.

Check that the master-cylinder level is correct. If it is not, top it up. Now get your assistant to depress the pedal a full stroke, letting it spring back as quickly as he can. As he starts to press the pedal, open the bleed screw three-quarters of a turn. Fluid will be ejected through the pipe and into the jar. You will notice that it contains air bubbles, the cause of your troubles. Keep an eye on the fluid while your assistant continues to pump. When the fluid leaves the pipe clear, with no sign of aeration, you can re-tighten the bleed screw. Do this during a down stroke of the brake pedal.

Repeat the operation with all the remaining bleed nipples, finishing at that nearest the master cylinder, i.e. the off-side front one. Do not over-tighten the nipples, which seat on cones. Use a 4–5 in. long spanner and torque them to between 5 and $7\frac{1}{2}$ lb ft if possible.

Finally, re-check the level of hydraulic fluid in the master-cylinder and top it up with fresh fluid if necessary. Do not use the fluid from the jar. That is contaminated. You can, if you wish, retain this for use in bleeding. It can also be used again if it is allowed to stand for several days until all the air has disappeared. For my part, however, I never use old brake fluid again.

Flushing the Hydraulic System. Once every couple of years the hydraulic system should be drained and flushed. This is done in a way rather similar to bleeding the system, except that only one nipple is involved and it is left open all the time.

Connect up the bleed tube, run it into a large jar, open the bleed nipple, and pump at the pedal until all fluid in the system has been expelled. Then pour in either special brake flushing fluid or industrial methylated spirits (*not* ordinary household meths) and pump this through also.

Next, pour in fresh brake fluid. Allow it to remain in the system for a while, then pump it all out. This will bring with it the remains of the flushing medium. The system is now clean, and can be refilled with fresh brake fluid and bled in the normal way.

Adjusting the Front Brakes. The brakes being in everyday use, the deterioration in their power is constant but gradual. Consequently, the average driver tends to become accustomed to a steadily-reducing braking power and does not realize when the time has come to adjust the brakes. For this reason, I suggest that a braking test is made weekly.

Choose a quiet stretch of road, and a convenient marker point. After the brakes have been adjusted, drive up to the marker at 30 m.p.h., apply the brakes, and note where the car stops. Repeat this at weekly intervals,

FIG. 77. BRAKE SHOE ADJUSTMENT

A special spanner, several types of which are obtainable from accessory shops, is required to turn the small square-headed adjusters provided for adjusting the front and rear brake shoes.

and you will have a yardstick by which to judge your braking power. When the stopping distance becomes significantly longer it is time to adjust the brakes again.

Brake adjustment is done by means of cams which move the shoes closer to the brake-drum. There are two adjusters for each front brake. To turn them you will need a special spanner, which is not supplied with the car. Most accessory shops stock them.

Jack up the front of the car until the wheels clear the ground. Then place blocks under the front suspension, at the centre of the car, so that it cannot topple. Engage the spanner with one of the squared adjusters, and turn it *anti-clockwise* until it is fully retracted (*see* Fig. 77). Do this with the second adjuster also.

Now turn one adjuster clockwise until it locks. This shows that the brake shoe is hard against the drum. Slacken the adjuster by two clicks on its built-in locking device and the wheel should spin freely when rotated by hand. Repeat the sequence with the second adjuster; then deal similarly with the two adjusters on the other front brake. You can then remove the blocks and lower the car.

Adjusting the Rear Brakes. Before jacking up the rear of the car for adjusting the rear brakes, place chocks against the front wheels so that the vehicle will not roll. Then jack up and block the rear end, having first ensured that the handbrake is off.

There is *one* adjuster for each rear brake. Turn the brake adjuster clockwise until it locks. Here, again, it shows that the shoes are hard against the brake-drum. Slacken it by two clicks and you should obtain free rotation. Repeat the sequence with the other rear brake; remove the blocks; lower the car; apply the handbrake; and unchock the front wheels.

Adjusting the Handbrake. In the normal way, merely adjusting the rear brakes automatically sets the hand brake as well. There is, however, an independent adjustment which can be brought into use if there is excessive hand-brake travel after the rear brakes have been accurately set. Release the hand-brake lever; chock the front wheels; jack up the rear of the car; and insert blocks under the rear frame member. Using the special spanner, turn both rear-brake adjusters *clockwise* until all four shoes are hard against the drums.

Now slide underneath the car and remove the eight bolts, with washers, holding the cover plate to the centre floor-assembly. There you will find the twin cables which actuate the hand-brake levers on the brakes. Set each cable individually, screwing up its adjusting nut until all slack is removed. During this operation the cable must be held steady by engaging a small spanner on the small hexagon which is located near the front of the cable on the side opposite to the adjuster.

When both cables are properly set, replace the cover plate. The end with the upturned tongue must be fitted towards the front of the car. Tighten the eight securing bolts, and then re-adjust the rear brake shoes in the normal way.

RENEWING BRAKE SHOES

The Front Shoes. Periodically the condition of the linings on the brake shoes must be inspected by detaching the brake drums. To remove each front brake-drum, first remove the nave plate and loosen the wheel nuts. Then jack up the car; insert blocks below the front suspension; and remove the wheel. Next slacken the two brake adjusters completely, and remove the single countersunk-screw in the face of the drum. The drum can then be pulled off.

If the linings have become worn down to rivet level, or are contaminated with grease, they must be changed. The best way is to purchase a factory-reconditioned set of replacement shoes—a little more expensive than fixing linings yourself, but unquestionably safer.

Detach the old shoes first. This entails removal of the leaf springs and steady posts mid-way along each shoe. Hold the head of the post, compress the spring, and slide the spring sideways. Then lift the shoe out of engagement with the wheel-cylinder slot and free the pull-off spring from the back plate. It is hooked into place. Do the same with the other shoe, and to protect the hydraulics against possible damage, slip strong rubber bands endwise round them, so that if the brake pedal happens to be depressed accidentally the pistons will not be shot out of the cylinders.

Fitting the new shoes is basically a simple reversal of removal procedure, but there are several points worth noting. One is that the slot in the wheel cylinder should be smeared with Girling White Brake Grease. Under no circumstances use ordinary solid lubricants at this point.

Note, too, that the pull-off springs fit behind the brake shoe web, with the hook on each spring inserted into the hole drilled adjacent to the steady post. The manufacturers recommend that when new shoes are fitted one should also renew the springs. Finally, when re-inserting the leaf springs fit them with their open ends towards the end of the pull-off spring.

When the new shoes have been fitted and the drum replaced, re-adjust each brake in the normal way, but slacken off the two adjusters by *three clicks* instead of two. This is a precaution to allow for expansion of the lining. After both brakes have been allowed to settle down for a while, revert to the standard settings.

The Rear Shoes. Follow the normal procedure of removing the nave plate, loosening the wheel nuts, chocking the front wheels, jacking and blocking the car and removing the rear wheels. The rear brake-drum too is held by a single countersunk screw and can be pulled off after this has been removed and the shoe adjuster racked off.

Then remove the shoes from each rear brake-drum as follows. Remove the slotted washer, coil spring and steady post from one shoe. To do this one must again hold the head of the post. Then depress the washer and rotate it a quarter of a turn, working against the pressure of the coil spring. Detach the washer and spring, and repeat on the other shoe.

Note which end of which spring fits into which hole in each shoe (a rough sketch is a useful aid when it comes to re-assembling) and then free the heel of the rearmost brake shoe from the slot in the adjuster at the top of the plate. Next, ease its lower end away from the cylinder. This will release the pressure of the pull-off springs and enable you to detach the front shoe too. Here, again, protect the cylinder by fitting an elastic band endwise round it to hold the piston securely.

As with the front brakes, lubricate the slots in the wheel cylinder and in the adjuster links with Girling White Brake Grease, and re-assemble with new pull-off springs. Of these, the single-coil spring fits inside the shoe webs, next to the adjuster, using the inner of the two holes so that the tips of the springs locate in the outer holes. The double-coil spring goes outside the brake-shoe webs, adjacent to the wheel cylinder, and in this case the longer coil is hooked to the front brake-shoe, using the outer of the two holes at each end.

Reassemble the rest of the brake by reversing the dismantling sequence and make the normal adjustment, but setting the adjuster *three clicks* out until the brakes have been properly bedded down.

GIRLING SERVO UNITS

Where a servo is fitted, one extra maintenance job should be carried out at intervals of 5,000 miles. This is to renew the unit's air filter, which is contained under a cylindrical cover on top of the servo.

A single central screw holds the filter cover. Release this and lift the cover. Discard the air filter element inside, but retain the rubber sealing washer. Clean the washer, the filter base plate, and the cover itself. Then place the washer on the base plate, followed by the new filter, and refit the cover.

Removal of servo unit. Provided the following sequence is observed there should be no difficulty in removing and refitting the servo. The steps are:

1 Disconnect the vacuum hose by withdrawing the banjo bolt on the servo unit. Discard the banjo's two sealing washers, since these must always be renewed if the unit has been disturbed.
2 Detach the hydraulic pipes from the servo's inlet and outlet ports. Place a tray underneath before loosening the unions, since fluid will escape as they are undone.
3 Undo the three mounting bolts and lift the servo unit from its bracket.
4 Reverse the sequence to refit the unit. When doing so remember to fit a new sealing washer to each side of the banjo union. When the unit is fully reconnected—*but before the engine has been restarted*—bleed the hydraulic system. This job *must* be done at this stage, since starting the engine will activate the vacuum-controlled servo and the brake pedal movement will then seal the high- and low-pressure sections of the servo system from each other. It is impossible to bleed the system properly once this has happened.

Later-type Servo Unit. This unit—the Girling Mark IIB—can be recognized by the design of the main vacuum chamber. Earlier models had a chamber with a bolted-on back plate. The later type has a two-piece shell joined by a concentric retaining band. With this unit, renewal is advised after 40,000 miles use.

Two servicing kits are available. As with the earlier servo, the air filter element must be replaced at 5,000-mile intervals. The procedure is exactly the same as that already described. In addition, the non-return valve is easily replaceable. This is the unit to which the vacuum hose from the inlet manifold attaches. To renew it, release the hose and use a stout screwdriver to lever the valve out of place in the grommet in which it seats. When doing this, it is vital to ensure that the grommet is not pushed into the vacuum chamber.

When the valve and grommet have been removed, fit a new grommet to the shell and then grease the ribs of the replacement valve body. Special grease for this purpose is provided with the Girling replacement kit, and no other type should be used. Then press the valve fully home in the grommet, and reconnect the vacuum hose.

Removal and refitting. This unit is removed simply by detaching the vacuum hose and the hydraulic pipes, and undoing the four bolts that hold the servo and its mounting bracket to the car. The bracket can be detached from the servo, if necessary, by undoing its three mounting screws. After refitting (a reversal of removal) follow the normal brake bleeding procedure.

PIPES, HOSES, CABLES

Inspection of Pipes and Hoses. No other work is advisable on the braking system, but a careful check should be kept on the condition of all pipes and hoses; any which have deteriorated should be renewed immediately. If the car is used on the road every day, it is no bad scheme to have all hoses and pipes renewed at intervals of, say, three years.

Where a union is "weeping," it can be tightened by the use of a short spanner (4–5 in. long at the most). Do not overtighten, for there is a danger of stripping its threads. If the unions can be set with a torque wrench, use a loading of 7 to 8 lb ft on male unions and 8 to 10 lb ft on female.

Renewing Handbrake Cables. Work, initially, as if adjusting the cables. Remove the end of each cable from the wheel-cylinder lever, discarding the split-pin (a new one should be used on reassembly), removing the plain and spring washers, and withdrawing the clevis pin from the lever eye.

Free the two bolts which clamp each cable to the rear-suspension arm and underneath the body detach each of the adjuster nuts. The cables can then be pulled rearward through the slide in the main cross-member. When fitting new cables, feed them through the slide from the rear but do not attach them to the handbrake lever until you have secured them to the wheel levers and the suspension arms. The washer and spring can then be slipped on to the threaded end of each cable, which should then be inserted through the lever boss. Refit the adjuster nuts and make a normal handbrake adjustment.

11 Work on the body

ODDLY enough, drivers who would never tolerate a noisy or a rough control action seem quite prepared to let body rattles or draughty windows go by default, although a little time spent on body maintenance would eliminate such annoyance. Usually this work is quite straightforward.

Facia Removal. Before attempting to detach the facia, disconnect the earthed terminal from the battery, so that there is no danger of short-circuiting the wiring. Then the instrument binnacle can be removed. It is held to the facia rail by two bolts, reached from below and set one at each end of the binnacle frame. In addition, two bolts hold it to a bracket fixed to a boss above the steering column. Take out these four bolts and move the binnacle sufficiently to enable you to release the instrument cables and wiring.

The remaining section of the facia is the filler panel, set on the passenger side of the car. It is held by two screws which are normally concealed below spire caps. Lift these caps, undo the screws, take out the ash-tray (a push-in fit) and pull out the panel. This removal procedure applies to all but a few early cars where the panel was held by pegs engaging in rubber-lined sockets. A few cars may also have screws set along the lower forward-edge of the panel. Check this point before attempting to pull it away.

Curing Facia Rattles. On some Imps facia rattle may be encountered. To obviate it the manufacturers have introduced several modifications which can easily be included on all cars prone to facia rattle.

One test to determine the cause of facia rattle is to grasp the instrument binnacle and attempt to rock it vertically when this is done. Should it tend to move when this is done a special stiffener needs to be linked between the binnacle and the facia rail. This stay (Part No. 7200721) is merely screwed into place, a hole being drilled in the rail to accommodate it. When drilling, be sure that the drill is not allowed to damage any of the wiring under the facia rail. Some cars already have a cage-nut fitted here to take the stiffener. If so, it should be used. On the binnacle an existing hole can be utilized.

On the lower edge of the binnacle the latest-type support stay should be fitted. This has a gusset on its upper face, which is missing from the earlier stays, and has been used from chassis No. B 41 1019406 on de luxe models

and from chassis No. B 42 1000183 on standard cars. The stay's Part No.
is 7200565 or 7200566 for right-hand or left-hand drive cars respectively.

Facia Replacement. To replace both the filler panel and the binnacle it
is necessary only to reverse the stripping procedure described on page 109.
Be certain that any wires which have been detached are duly refitted in
their proper places.

New facia finishers (rubber gaskets) should be used for both the binnacle
and the filler. Under the binnacle, this finisher should be fitted with its
widest leg (that with a large hole in it), set towards the centre line of the
car and with the deeper flange on the driver's side. On the filler panel the
existing finishing strip should be discarded. Left-hand finishers are
Part No. 7200537 L/H; right-hand finishers Part No. 7200538 R/H. They
are best attached to the facia rail with Dunlop S. 758 adhesive.

Switch Rattles. There are several methods of eliminating rattles caused
by the ignition/starter switch. One is to use washers against the bottom
shoulder of the lock barrel, and for this Chrysler can supply both plastic and
sponge-rubber types, known respectively by the Part Nos. 7102434 and
7102487. In addition, use of an MS 4 silicone-based grease on the lock
barrel will help to cure unwanted noises, and will also have the side-effect
of lubricating the wards of the lock.

Door Adjustment. The doors can be set further into the body by moving
the striker plate fitted to each door pillar. The striker plate is held by
three screws. Before loosening these, mark round the plate with a pencil
to establish its original position as a reference. Then loosen the screws
sufficiently to enable the plate to be moved, and press it inwards by about
$\frac{1}{8}$ in. Tighten the three screws and check the effect of the adjustment. It
can then be altered, in similar easy stages, until the door seats hard against
its rubbers, yet shuts without any difficulty.

Door Seals. These combined seals and "furflex" piping are retained
solely by small metal tags concealed within the seal itself. Pull on the seal
to remove it. When refitting the seal you may find that it is necessary to tap
the piping with a block of wood to ensure that the seal is fully home.

Squeaking from the doors may be due to scarcely perceptible movement
between the door frame and the seals. It can be alleviated by coating the
rubber seals with a silicone spray or by the application of a wax pencil.
This will have to be repeated at intervals.

Door Lubrication. Periodically apply a little oil to the door hinge-pins.
The door locks will also require oiling. When doing this, wind the
windows fully up and leave the doors wide open. After oil has been injected
onto the locking mechanism, leave the doors open as long as possible.

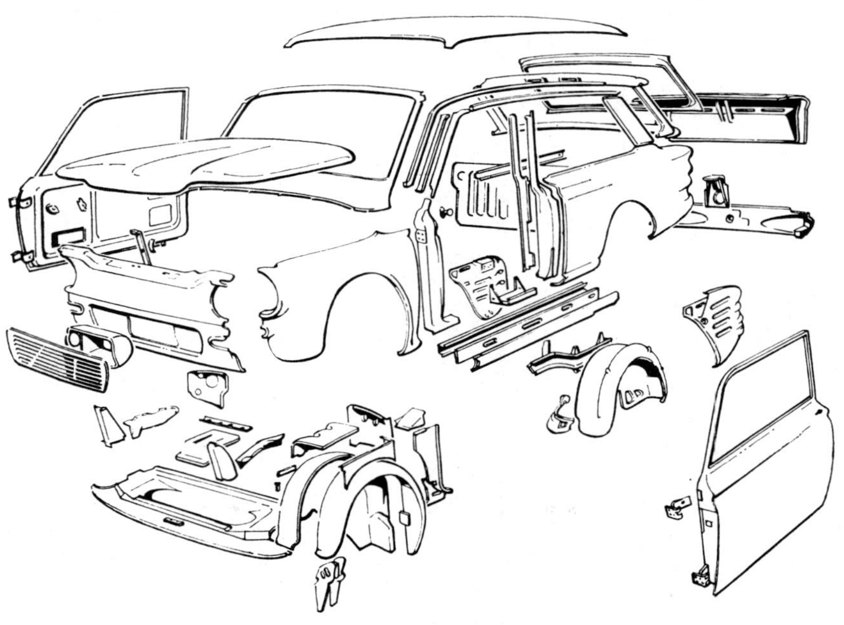

Fig. 78. The Imp Body Layout

The Imp body, primarily a welded steel structure, comprises many different pressings and parts. Their co-relationship is shown above.

This enables "waste" oil to drain away through the door drain holes without entering the car interior.

The push-button lock control can be lubricated by injecting thin oil around the button, working from outside the car. For lubricating the wards of the lock the makers recommend the use of Shell Silicone Compound. A little of this should be placed on the key, which is then inserted into the lock. The lock should be operated a few times and the key then withdrawn. Wipe off any surplus compound. Oil can be injected in the same way if no compound is available.

Door Handles [Interior]. The interior door handles can be removed simply by driving out the retaining pins. To do this, turn each handle's escutcheon plate (the plastic plate behind the handle) until the groove in it matches up with the dowel hole in the handle itself. Then, using an awl, tap out securing pin and remove the handle and escutcheon. Replacement is a reversal of this procedure.

Door Trim. After detaching the door handles, remove the screws which secure the door pockets (not fitted to standard models or on some cars overseas). The screws holding the lower end of the trim can then be taken out and the panel freed from its retaining tongue at the door waist. It will first be necessary to press it upwards to clear the spindles of the door-lock control and the window regulator. Then pull it downwards to detach.

When refitting, place the top edge of the panel under its tongue first. Until it is properly seated, the rest of the locations should not be made.

Door Handles [Exterior]. Before the external handle can be reached the trim panel must be removed from the door's inner face, giving access to the door casing. The door-handle nuts can then be detached and the handle eased out, taking care not to lose the seating washers set between the handle and the outer door panel.

Door Push-button Adjustment. The door lock is actuated through a plunger attached to the push-button in the door handle, and this can be adjusted. Remove the trim and insert a feeler gauge between the head of the plunger and the lock contactor. The clearance here should be $\frac{1}{32}$ in. (0·031 in. or 0·79 mm). If an adjustment is required, release the lock-nut and rack the plunger in or out. Tighten the lock-nut and recheck the clearance before replacing the trim.

Window Removal. Detach the trim and then take out the screws securing the bottom-stop bracket low down and slightly aft of centre of the door. Remove the inner and outer waist seals from the lower edge of the window aperture and detach the window regulator.

This is done by temporarily replacing the window winding-handle and lowering the glass to roughly its half-way position, where it must be

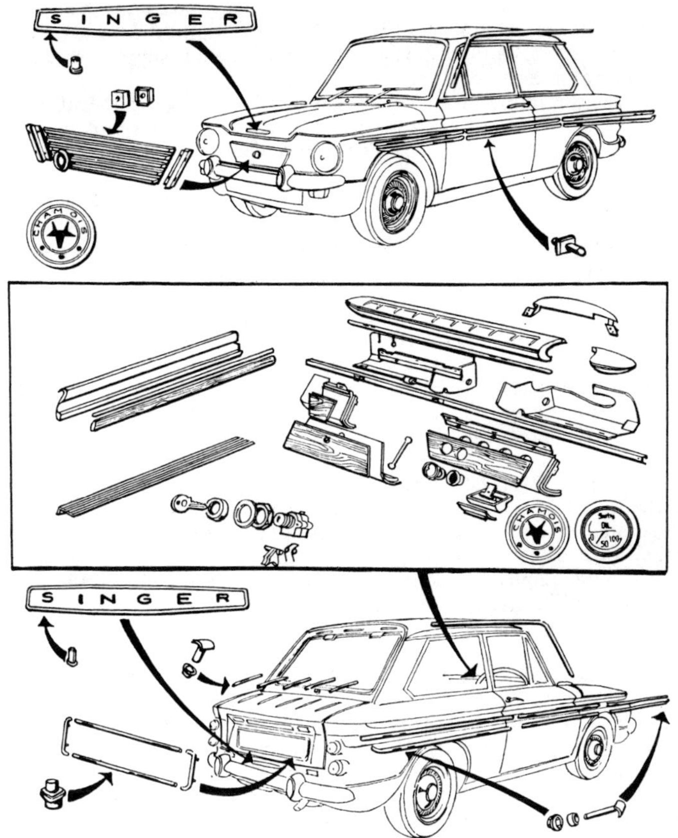

FIG. 79. THE SINGER CHAMOIS TRIMMINGS
The detailed sketches show how the various trimmings are secured.

supported by a block of wood. Now undo the three screws set in a triangle around the window winder-spindle. Slide the regulator's operating arm out of the bottom channel, and lift it out of the door aperture. The window can then be lowered to the bottom of the door.

Leaving it there temporarily, ease the front glass run-channel out of its housing. Then turn the window so that its lower edge, complete with the cam-plate, is towards the *rear* edge of the door. Raise it gently and ease it out through its own operating aperture.

Window Replacement. Except that the inner and outer waist-seals should be fitted after the window has been replaced and set in its correct position, but *before* the regulator arm is located, replacement is simply a reversal of the removal procedure.

To ease the fitting of the small clips which hold the waist-seals at the lower edge of the door aperture, make up a hook from a piece of $\frac{1}{64}$ in. steel sheet 4 in. long and $\frac{1}{2}$ in. wide (1·5 mm × 10 cm × 12·7 mm).

Ventilator Removal. Before the ventilator (front quarter-light) can be detached the winding window has to be removed, as just described. Two screws (one at the upper and the other at the lower forward edges) hold the ventilator. With these removed, grasp the quarter-light by its rear top-edge and pull it towards the window aperture, freeing the lower swivel bracket as you do so. Refit it in the same way.

In the case of the fixed quarter-light, used on standard cars, there are no screws to remove, the light being held simply by its rubber surround and by the main window's front channelling. Apart from this the method of removal is identical to that when two screws are provided. And so, also, is the refitting procedure.

Rear Screen Removal. Open the rear screen fully, and arrange a sling so that it can be supported. Then mark both the lower stays so that you are certain they will be reassembled in the same position. This is vital, for if they are accidentally turned, the centre hinge will foul the screen as it is closed. Now remove the screws from each hinge at the top of the screen aperture, and release the lower set-screws from the stays. The complete screen can now be removed from the car.

Windscreen and Rear Quarter-Lights. There should be no need to detach any of the fixed glasses except in cases of breakages. Since refitting is a delicate job, requiring two operators, it is inadvisable to tackle it at home. The risk of breakage makes it an uneconomic proposition, and one which is better entrusted to professionals.

Where leakage occurs around the weather-stripping, however, repairs can be made without detaching the glass. After drying out any excess moisture, inject a sealing compound such as "Seelastik" right round the strip. The glass must be perfectly clean and dry, or it will not adhere.

Door Lock Removal. After detaching the interior handles and trim, remove the screws set in a triangle around the remote-control lock handle and the four screws on the rear face of the door and lift out the lock.

Bonnet Lock Removal. Release the control cable inside the bonnet, where it is clamped to the remote-control bracket, and detach the two screws above the front panel platform which hold the striker plate. The striker itself is held to the bonnet lid by two set-screws.

Bonnet Lock (Emergency Release). Should the remote control not function when the lid is closed, the lock can be operated by removing the front grille (held by two screws and tongues) and pushing out the large grommet set in the top of the heater air-intake. The remote-control bracket can then be pushed to the left to free the bonnet.

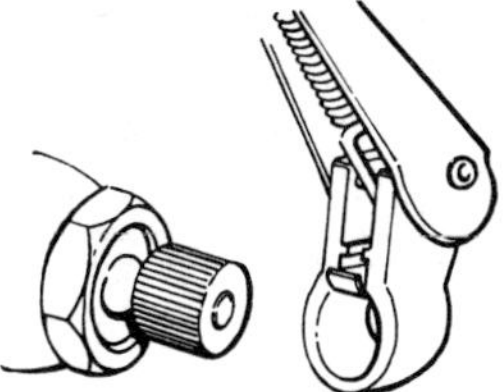

FIG. 80. WINDSCREEN WIPER ARM REMOVAL

Each wiper arm fits on splines on the spindle and is retained by the blade-type springs set in the arm. Lift this free. If the blade rides over the screen surround, reset it higher.

Engine Lid Locks. With the lid raised, detach the lock-nut and the nut which secures the exterior handle. Some cars have only one nut at this point. Then detach the two screws which hold the lock to the lid.

Rear Screen Lock Removal. First detach the bezel of the lock, with its sealing washer, by straightening the tags from the underside. Next remove, from the interior face of the frame, the four screws which hold the lock.

Headlining. Private owners would be well advised *not* to attempt replacement of the headlining. It is a skilled job, if the original appearance is to be maintained, and removal of the existing lining requires the windscreen and both rear quarter-lights to be detached.

Seat Removal. The front seats can be freed by removing the seat assembly retaining-bolts at the front corners and lifting them out. The rear seat cushion is removed simply by lifting its front face clear of the retaining valance. To detach the rear-seat squab, remove the set-screws which hold the pivots to the wheel arches, being careful not to damage the trim. When replacing these screws, treat them with "Seelastik."

Body Mouldings, etc. The name plates and badges are held simply by spring retaining-clips, and can be levered off. The same applies to the rear quarter mouldings and the engine-compartment lid moulding. They can be eased up with a piece of wood sharpened to a thin wedge shape at one end. The bonnet side and door mouldings are also held by clips, but with one pop rivet, in addition, which must be drilled out. When refitting the trim, any used plastic clips *must* be replaced with new parts.

Appendix

<table>
<tr><td colspan="2" align="center">OIL, FUEL, WATER CAPACITIES</td></tr>
<tr><td>Sump and filter</td><td>5½ pints (6·6 U.S. pints; 3·1 litres)</td></tr>
<tr><td>Sump, filter and oil cooler</td><td>6 pints (7·2 U.S. pints; 3·4 litres)</td></tr>
<tr><td>Transaxle</td><td>4½ pints (5·5 U.S. pints; 2·5 litres)</td></tr>
<tr><td>Steering unit</td><td>½ pint (0·7 U.S. pint; 0·28 litre)</td></tr>
<tr><td>Petrol tank</td><td>6 gals. (7·2 U.S. gals.; 27·2 litres)</td></tr>
<tr><td>Cooling system and heater
  From engine No. B.411015433
  Earlier engines</td><td>
10¼ pints (12·3 U.S. pints; 5·8 litres)
11 pints (13·2 U.S. pints; 6·2 litres)</td></tr>
</table>

<table>
<tr><td colspan="2" align="center">RECOMMENDED LUBRICANTS</td></tr>
<tr><td>The Imp Engine
  Below 5°F (−15°C)</td><td>Shell X 100 Multigrade 5W/20</td></tr>
<tr><td> 0—32°F (−18 to 0°C)</td><td>Shell X 100 10 W or as above</td></tr>
<tr><td> 20° to 68°F (−7 to 27°C)</td><td>Shell X 100 20 W or Multigrade 10W/30</td></tr>
<tr><td> Above 68°F (above 20°C)</td><td>Shell X 100 30 or Multigrade 20W/40</td></tr>
<tr><td> Continuous high speed</td><td>Shell X 100 Multigrade 20W/40 or
  Shell X 100/40</td></tr>
<tr><td>Transaxle</td><td>Shell Spirax 80 EP (75 EP below 5°F or
  −15°C)</td></tr>
<tr><td>Steering</td><td>Shell Spirax 80 EP</td></tr>
<tr><td>Swivel pins</td><td>Shell Retinax A or Shell Spirax 140EP</td></tr>
<tr><td>Brake and clutch fluid reservoir</td><td>Girling Brake Fluid (Spec. S.A.E. 70R.3)</td></tr>
<tr><td>Wheel bearings</td><td>Shell Retinax A</td></tr>
<tr><td>Distributor</td><td>Engine oil (shaft and cam bearing; contact-breaker pivot; automatic timing control) Shell Retinax A (cam profile)</td></tr>
<tr><td>Dynamo</td><td>Engine oil</td></tr>
<tr><td>Body (hinges, etc.)</td><td>Engine oil</td></tr>
<tr><td>Battery terminals</td><td>Silicone grease</td></tr>
</table>

* The engine oil recommendations are for the prevailing climatic temperature ranges specified. If an upper cylinder lubricant is used, Shell U.C.L. is suggested. The manufacturers stress that no additive of any sort should be used in the transaxle.

TECHNICAL DETAILS OF IMP ENGINE

Bore	67·99/67·98 mm (2·6769/2·6766 in.) Grade A 68/67·99 mm (2·6772/2·6769 in.) Grade B 68·01/68 mm (2·6775/2·6772 in.) Grade C
Stroke	60·37 mm (2·377 in.)
Capacity (standard bore)	875 cc (53·4 cu in.)
Compression ratio	10 to 1 (standard); 8 to 1 (low)
Compression pressure	185/200 lb per sq in. (13/14 kg per sq cm)
Tappet clearance (cold)	0·004/0·006 in. (0·10/0·15 mm) inlet 0·006/0·008 in. (0·15/0·20 mm) exhaust
Timing (valve)	Inlet opens 6° B.T.D.C., closes 46° A.B.D.C. Exhaust opens 46° B.B.D.C., closes 6° A.T.D.C.
Piston diameter	67·965/67·957 mm (2·6758/2·6755 in.) Grade A 67·972/67·965 mm (2·6761/2·6758 in.) Grade B 67·98/67·972 mm (2·6764/2·6761 in.) Grade C 67·987/67·980 mm (2·6767/2·6764 in.) Grade D
Oversizes available	0·38 mm (0·015 in.) and 0·76 mm (0·030 in.)
Skirt clearance	0·0014/0·0008 in. (0·035/0·020 mm) at right-angles to the gudgeon-pin
Ring clearance (vertical, in groove)	0·0035/0·0015 in. (0·088/0·037 mm)
Ring gap (fitted, in Grade A bore)	0·0013/0·008 in. (0·33/0·20 mm)
Timing chain	Single-row roller, 0·375 in. (9·5 mm) pitch × 82 links; 0·25 in. (6·3 mm) roller dia.; 0·225 in. (5·71 mm) width
End float (crankshaft)	0·002/0·01 in. (0·05/0·25 mm)
(camshaft)	0·007/0·002 in. (0·17/0·05 mm)
Oil pressure (hot)	50 lb per sq in. (3·5 kg per sq cm)
Filter	Tecalemit full-flow, 1 pt (1·2 U.S. pints; 0·57 litre) capacity
Radiator cap	7 lb per sq in. (from B.41/1003496 & B.42/1000101) 4 lb per sq in. (early models)
Thermostat	Opens at 170/179°F (77/80°C)
Fan belt	43·62 in. (110·8 cm) outside length; 40° Vee; 0·31 in. (7·9 mm) depth; 0·375 in. (9·5 mm) outer width
Firing order	1–3–4–2 (No. 1 cylinder at front)
Ignition timing (nominal, static	3° (3 mm) B.T.D.C.
Distributor type	Lucas 25.D.4
Rotation	Anti-clockwise
Contact-breaker gap	0·015 in. (0·38 mm)
Coil	Lucas HA12 or 11 C12 (BA7, export)
Recommended plugs	Champion N9Y
Plug gap	0·025 in.
Output	42 b.h.p. gross (39 net) at 5,000 r.p.m.
Torque	52 lb ft. at 2,800 r.p.m.
Fuel pump pressure	$1\frac{1}{4}$/2 lb per sq in. (0·08/0·14 kg per sq cm)

CARBURETTOR COMPONENT	SOLEX CARBURETTOR SETTINGS		
	B30 PIHT	B30 PIHT–2	B30 PIHT–3
Choke	22 mm	20 mm	20 mm
Main jet	112·5	102/105	102
Econstat jet	60	80	80
Pilot jet	45	40	40
Pilot jet air-bleed	100	80	1·4
Air correction	160	150	150
Progression holes	1 × 1·2	2 × 1·2	—
Needle-valve seat	1·3	1·6	1·6

(all with 1 mm paper washer fitted)

ZENITH-STROMBERG CARBURETTOR SETTINGS (125 CDS)

Metering needle	6K (B.17351Z), up to 5,000 ft. 5U(B.17751Z) 5,000–10,000 ft. 5V (B.17752Z) above 10,000 ft.
Damper spring	0·032
Fast-idle gap	0·9–1·0 mm at throttle
Slow-running speed	1,000 rpm

IMP BRAKE DRUMS

Drum diameter	8 in. (20·3 cm)
Lining width	1·5 (38·1 mm)
Lining material	Don 202 (MS 3 on later cars)

STEERING AND SUSPENSION

Toe-in (at tyre tread)	$\frac{3}{16}$ in. plus or minus $\frac{1}{8}$ in.
Castor angle	10° plus or minus 1°, positive
Camber angle	$7\frac{1}{2}$° plus or minus 1°, positive
King-pin inclination	$3\frac{1}{2}$° plus or minus 1°, positive
Ackermann angle	Nil
Rear toe-in (at tyre tread)	$\frac{5}{16}$ in. plus or minus $\frac{1}{8}$ in.
Rear camber angle	$\frac{1}{2}$° plus or minus 45° positive

Wheels and Tyres

Front hub end-float	0·0065/0·003 in. (0·165/0·076 mm)
Wheels	Steel disc; 12L × 4J or 4½J; four stud
Tyres recommended	5·50 × 12 Dunlop C.41 or 155 × 12 Tubeless Dunlop SP41
Rolling radius	10·45 in. (front); 10·57 in. (rear)
Tyre pressures	
front	18 lb per sq in. (1·3 kg per sq cm)
rear	30 lb per sq in. (2·1 kg per sq cm)
spare	30 lb per sq in. (2·1 kg per sq cm)

Correct Lucas Bulbs for Lamps, etc.

Headlamp (U.K.)	No. 5041043 light unit bulb (r.h.d.)
Headlamp (France)	No. 411 (l.h.d.)
Headlamp (North America)	No. 7105078 light unit (l.h.d.)
Side light	No. 989(12V 6W) or No. 222 (12V 4W)
Stop and tail light	No. 380 (12V 21/6W)
Front and rear flashers	No. 382 (12V 21W)
Rear number-plate	No. 207 (12V 6W)
Interior	No. 254 (12V 6W festoon)
Panel	No. 987 (12V 2·2W)
Main beam indicator	No. 987 (12V 2·2W)
Ignition warning	No. 987 (12V 2·2W)
Flasher warning	No. 987 (12V 2·2W)
Oil pressure warning	No. 987 (12V 2·2W)

Torque Settings (Engine)

Cylinder-head bolts (*cold*)	36 lb ft (5 kg m)
Main bearing-cap bolts	41 lb ft (5·6 kg m)
Big-end bolts	18 lb ft (2·4 kg m)
Bell-housing studs	9 lb ft (1·2 kg m)
Camshaft bearing-cap nuts	6 lb ft (0·8 kg m)
Sparking plugs	14 lb ft (1·9 kg m)
Camshaft sprocket set-screw	19 lb ft (2·6 kg m)
Flywheel/crankshaft bolts	32 lb ft (4·4 kg m)
Temperature switch body	20 lb ft (2·7 kg m)
All $\frac{1}{4}$ in. UNF stud nuts	6 lb ft (0·8 kg m)
All $\frac{5}{16}$ in. stud nuts	15 lb ft (2·0 kg m)
All other parts	6 lb ft (0·8 kg m)

TORQUE SETTINGS (TRANSMISSION)

Drive-shaft flange nuts	105 lb ft (14·5 kg m)
Bell-housing nuts	25 lb ft (3·5 kg m)
Clutch release-lever nut	11 lb ft (1·5 kg m)
Rear-hub nut	170 lb ft (23·5 kg m)
Rotoflex-coupling bolts	34 lb ft (4·7 kg m)
Clutch/flywheel bolts	7 lb ft (0·9 kg m)

TORQUE SETTINGS (SUSPENSION, STEERING, ETC.)

King-pin carrier/wishbone	
(horizontal)	74 lb ft (10·2 kg m)
(vertical)	48 lb ft (6·6 kg m)
Wishbone pivot-bolts	25 lb ft (3·4 kg m)
Suspension support-brackets	27 lb ft (3·7 kg m)
Wheel nuts	48 lb ft (6·6 kg m)
Shock absorber/suspension mounting	
(front)	43 lb ft (5·9 kg m)
(rear)	25 lb ft (3·4 kg m)
Shock absorber/body mounting	
(front)	20 lb ft (2·7 kg m)
(rear)	14 lb ft (1·9 kg m)
King-pin retainer nut	6 lb ft (0·8 kg m) flat square with taper
Front-hub locknut	13 lb ft (1·7 kg m)
Rear suspension pivot-bolts	43 lb ft (5·9 kg m)
Steering rack " U " bolts	14 lb ft (1·9 kg m)
Rack/track-rod bolts	53 lb ft (7·3 kg m)
Ball joints	20 lb ft (2·7 kg m)
Steering arm/stub axle	33 lb ft (4·5 kg m)
Inner column pinch-bolt:–	
$\frac{1}{4}$ in. UNF (head unmarked)	8 lb ft (1·1 kg m)
$\frac{1}{4}$ in. UNF (head marked V)	10 lb ft (1·4 kg m)
$\frac{5}{16}$ in. UNF (through bolt)	13 lb ft (1·7 kg m)
Brake back-plate/stub axle	14 lb ft (1·9 kg m)
Wheel cylinder/back-plate	6 lb ft (0·8 kg m)
Rear cross-member to body	27 lb ft (3·7 kg m)
Engine mounting/cross-member	27 lb ft (3·7 kg m)

Index

AIR filter, removal, 29, 30

BATTERY: charge, 66; corrosion, 66; topping-up, 65

Big-ends: bearing-shells, 43; cap bolts, torque, 45, 119; refitting, 45; renewal, 43; tab washers, 43

Brake: pipes, checking, 108; removal, 107, 108; servicing, 107; servo, Girling, 107

Brakes: bleeding, 103; fluid level, 102; flushing, 103; front, adjustment, 104; rear adjustment, 105; shoes, renewal, 105, 106

CAM cover, removal, 31

Camshaft: drive, reconnecting, 41; drive, releasing, 32, 34; refitting, 40; removal, 32, 33; retiming, 41

Carburettor, Solex: adjusting, 78, 81; automatic choke, 83, 84; cleaning, 82; components, 85; exploded, 81; sections, 79; servicing, 74, 78, 86

Carburettor, Stromberg: 86; air filter, elements, 94; cleaning, 92; components, 87; cross-section, 89; diaphragm location, 92; diaphragm removal, 92; exploded, 90; idling adjustment, 87; jets, 86; linkages, 88; piston stop, 93; starter, 91

Centrifugal advance, dismantling, 59

Clutch: refitting, 51; release bearing, noisy, 42; release bearing, removal, 52; removal, 48

Contact-breaker: access, 57; exploded, 57; points, adjustment, 8, 9; points, cleaning, 57

Cooling system: draining, 35, 69; flushing, 69

Crankshaft: refitting, 50; removal, 49

Cylinder head: bolts, tightening, 36, bolts, torque, 40, 119; dummy stud, 40; refitting, 40; removal, 35; decarbonizing, 37

DAMPERS, front, attachment, 101

Decarbonizing, 28, 29

Distributor: exploded, 58; maintenance, 56; overhauling, 58; reassembly, 59; rebushing, 59; removal, 50; retiming, 55

Door handles: exterior, removal, 112; interior, removal, 112

Door: push-button, adjustment, 112; seals, fitting, 110; trim, removal, 112

Doors: adjustment, 110; lubrication, 110

Drive: camshaft, 4; distributor, 4; oil pump, 4

Drive couplings: bolts, torque, 54, 120; refittting, 54; removal, 53, 54

Dynamo: armature recutting, 61, 62; brushes, minimum length, 61; brushes, refitting, 62; brushes, renewal, 61; commutators, types, 61; dismantling, 60; exploded, 61; lubrication, 60; removal, 60

ENGINE: cleaning, 29; installing, 53; moving parts, 45; removal, 47; running-in, 10, 11; sectioned, 2, 3; stripping, 48

FACIA: curing rattles, 109; removal, 109; replacement, 110

Fan belt: grade, 55; setting, 10

Faults, diagnosis, 15

Flushing, reverse, 72

Flywheel, removal, 50

Fuel pipe, removal, 31

Fuel pump: diaphragm renewal, 75; exploded, 76; filter, checking, 75; gaskets, 30, 31; reassembly, 77; removal, 31; stripping, 75; troubles, 77

GEARBOX, sectioned, 5
Gudgeon pins; removal, 45; refitting, 46

HANDBRAKE: adjustment, 105; cable, renewing, 108
Headlamp, removing, 67
Heater: bleeding, 42, 69; control valve, 70
Hub nuts: security, 97; torque, 97, 120

IGNITION system, checking, 15

KINGPINS, greasing, 10

LIGHTING system, checking, 17
Lock, bonnet: emergency release, 115; removal, 114
Locks, doors, removal, 114

MAIN bearings: cap bolts, torque, 51, 119; rear, removal, 49; rear, seals, 50; replacing, 54
Maintenance, routine systems, 2, 3
Manifolds: refitting, 40; removal, 37

OIL: changes, engine 7; changes, transaxle, 8; cooler, disconnecting, 47; filter, renewal, 7; pump, refitting, 51; pump, removal, 49; topping-up, engine, 6; topping-up, transaxle, 8

PISTON rings, grooves, cleaning, 46
Pistons: decoke, 38, 39; diameters, 117; grades, 47; marking, 43; removal, 43
Pressure plate, removal, 48

RACK, steering: damper adjustment, 96; fixing nuts, 95; oil leakage, 95
Radiator: cleaning, 71; diagram, 72
Rear flasher lamp: bulb, 68, 119; removal, 68
Rear lamp: bulb, 68, 119; removal, 68
Ring gap: adjusting, 47; checking, 47; measurements, 47, 117
Rings, piston, fitting, 47

SCREEN, rear, removal, 114
Shims, valve, removal, 34
Side lamp: exploded, 67; bulbs, 67, 119; sealing, 67
Silencer, removal, 35
Small-end, bushes: inserting, 46; renewal, 45
Starter motor: Bendix drive, 65; brush removal, 64; commutator cleaning, 63; exploded, 64; rebuilding, 65; removal, 63; stripping, 63; testing, 63
Sump bolts, torque, 45, 119
Sump, removal, 43
Suspension, front: checking, 101; exploded, 100; rear, checking, 101

TAPPET block housing: refitting, 40; removal, 34, 35
Tappets, adjustment, 8, 32, 39, 40
Thermostat, 70–1
Throttle, cable, 86
Timing, method, 55
Track rod joints: removal, 96; renewal, 96
Tyre pressures, 96, 79, 119

VACUUM: advance, disconnecting, 59; pipe, removal, 37
Valve: clearances, checking, 31–2; clearances, setting, 32, 39, 117; gear, oilway, sealing ring, 36, 40; grinding method, 37
Valves: inlet, oil seals, 36, 37; removal, 37

WATER pump: bracket, 6; corrosion protection, 73; dismantling, 72; exploded, 73; reassembly, 73; removal, 72
Wheels, bearing: adjustment, 98; end float, 99; front, 98; lubrication, 99; rear, 99; run-out, 98
Wiring diagrams: Chamois, 20; Chamois Mk. 2, 22; Chamois Coupé, 24; Chamois Sport, 23; Chamois Coupé and Sport, 26; Husky Estate, 23, 27; Imp, 19; Imp Californian, 24, 25; Imp de Luxe, 21, 25; Imp Sport, 23, 26; Imp Super, 22, 25; Imp Van, 23, 27; Stiletto, 25, 27